THE WHISPER WITHIN

THE
WHISPER
WITHIN

RESTING IN OUR
CREATOR'S LOVE

LISA ENGELMAN

PARAKALEO
PRESS

Published by Parakaleo Press
Portland, Oregon, USA
Printed in the USA

Cover and interior design: InsideOut CreativeArts, Inc.

For additional information please visit https://parakaleopress.org/,
e-mail info@parakaleopress.org,
or write to P.O. Box 5844, Beaverton, OR 97006, USA.

To my selfless husband,
Stephen Engelman,
God's chosen vessel to show this sensitive soul
what His unconditional love and grace look like.

Thank you for loving me,
through the fullness of the Spirit in you,
as Christ loves the church
(see Eph. 5:25).

Being your bride has been
my greatest earthly blessing.

CONTENTS

FOREWORD

BY DR. JERRY RUEB

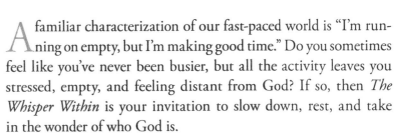

A familiar characterization of our fast-paced world is "I'm running on empty, but I'm making good time." Do you sometimes feel like you've never been busier, but all the activity leaves you stressed, empty, and feeling distant from God? If so, then *The Whisper Within* is your invitation to slow down, rest, and take in the wonder of who God is.

Sadly, too many Christians today ignore the warnings of living on the fumes of a faded faith. Jesus rocked the comfortable world of the Laodicean believers with these words: "I know your works: you are neither cold nor hot. Would that you were either cold or hot! So, because you are lukewarm, and neither hot nor cold, I will spit you out of my mouth. For you say, I am rich, I have prospered, and I need nothing, not realizing that you are wretched, pitiable, poor, blind, and naked" (Rev. 3:15–17, ESV). Christ's evaluation is all the more tragic because the Laodicean believers were deceived into thinking that everything was okay when, in fact, they were spiritually wretched, pitiable, poor, blind, and naked. In an effort to redirect them from disaster, Jesus called these active but empty believers to hear His voice again, open the doors of their hearts to allow Him to come in, and just be with Him.

Through the eyes of this book's author, Lisa Engelman, you will be introduced to a fresh encounter with Jesus through vivid colors of eternal truths and picturesque language. This biblically based book is devotional in tone and written in an inspirational quality reminiscent of authors like Andrew Murray, Oswald Chambers, F. B. Meyer, and A. W. Tozer. Like tiny boats cast about on the troubled waters of adversity, these writers spoke of the loving strength of their Anchor, the Lord Jesus Christ. This book relays the hard-fought insights of the author, who is an intrepid follower of Jesus, a faithful wife, a busy mother of four, a miraculous cancer survivor, and an author.

In *The Whisper Within*, get ready to go deeper, search harder, and walk more courageously up the steeper mountains of faith. As you walk, you will value the personal tone and the practical methodology of the "Pray It In" summaries at the end of each chapter. Keep walking, and you will find yourself scaling the mountains of pain, searching the dark valleys of suffering and doubt, and reaching the summits of faith and victory.

Discerning the voice of God amid the loud noises of the world as we journey through it requires a scout to show us the way. Lisa Engelman is a trusted guide who will lead you to the ultimate destination: at the feet of Jesus!

PREFACE

Every one of us knows what it's like to carry a burden. One weight I carried for many years was trying hard to please God. I loved Him, and I knew in my mind that He loved me. But my heart was stuck in an endless cycle of diligently checking every box on my daily spiritual to-do list; I yearned to know that God was proud of me. This led to self-effort, people pleasing, overwork, and, ultimately, exhaustion.

Your burden might be different from mine. Maybe you feel unloved, or you're lonely. Maybe you carry the heaviness of disappointment or regret or guilt, or perhaps you are grieving a great loss. You might be full of anxiety or fear. Maybe you're full of doubt as you struggle with parenting decisions. Or maybe you're just plain worn out by the increased busyness and expectations in our day from online programs and social networks that allege to draw us closer but in many ways divide us from each other.

In March 2018, the Lord drew me into a season of intentional prayer for revival in our land. Toward the end of that time, as I drove to a conference on August 25, 2018, God awakened my heart to His love and set me free from the load I was carrying. While savoring the time alone to pray in my car, I heard the Holy

Spirit's Whisper within: "*I love you. I love you. I love you.*" This experience transformed my life. For the first time, it sank into every part of my being how much God loved me. He loved me not because I was a perfect wife or momma or Christian. It was simply because *He is love.*

This experience was a beautiful fulfillment in my life of Romans 5:5: "We know how dearly God loves us, because he has given us the Holy Spirit to fill our hearts with his love." This fresh filling of the Holy Spirit swept away my weariness and disappointment and flooded my heart with joy.

In the days and weeks following, I drew near to the Lord in a new way. As I spent time with Jesus, I listened with new delight to His written voice, His Word, and also to His Whisper within me, quietly bringing truth alive to my heart and confirming His deep love for me. As I started to rest in God's great love, I stopped trying to do everything and please everyone. God began to show me what things *He* wanted me to do, and He supplied all the strength for it. What peace!

God wants us to be filled with His Holy Spirit (see Eph. 5:18). Yes, He has given us His Spirit as proof that we live in Him and He in us (see 1 John 4:13). His love waits for us to crack open the door of our hearts so He can flood our lives through His Spirit the moment we give our hearts to Jesus (see Rom. 5:5). But He also wants to give His people fresh, ongoing fillings of the Holy Spirit—the Spirit who is love.

As I observe our current Christian culture, it seems to me that there are often two general groups: those who place great emphasis on the Bible but have not yet experienced the fullness of the Holy Spirit and those who have experienced the gentle voice of the Holy Spirit but have strayed from being immersed in the written voice of God. One crowd murmurs that miracles don't happen now, and the other grievously reduces our great God to its own personal genie in a bottle. I am thankful to have been awakened to the

Whisper of the Holy Spirit within me, but the Word remains invaluable to me. To depart from the Word into the Spirit and not see them as *together*—I cannot resonate with that.

My new awareness of God's love sparked passion in me to experience more of this love that equips us to live with light hearts in a heavy world. I had to write this book, for the desire was bursting within me that others too would come and gaze upon our Jesus—and find rest for their souls. Return. Rest. Receive. Renew. Repeat. This is what so many of us who love Jesus desperately need today. As we slow down and fasten our eyes on Jesus, we can step into renewed lives, through His Spirit within us, of deep soul rest in our Savior's love.

Jesus wants us folded against Him, our shepherd, for in that place we are safe, sheltered, and quieted. His Spirit's Whisper within us can then move our souls from chaotic overload to unhurried moments of resting in our Creator's love.

Our culture has sped up to an unsustainable pace. Families are groaning under the weight of the increasing demands of our digital instant-everything culture. Many of us who love Jesus have lost a clear connection to our Father's voice—our Jesus by us, in us, inviting us to stay a while with Him. Just Him. We have started down the slippery slope of trading our eternal reward—God's approval—for a bit of man's praise "dopamine"[1] with each swipe of our phones. The energizing joy, renewal, and sharpness of mind that come in moments of solitude with the Lord are fading from our days.

I long to live in daily awareness of the triune dance of Father, Son, and Spirit that God set in motion from eternity past. We have a standing invitation to join in this dance and enjoy perfect fellowship with the Godhead! Just a taste of His triune love that ran red down the cross for us is all it takes for us to realize that we have found what we were created for: Him. Him. Him. Fervent tears are falling now from my eyes with desire for all God's people to know the Whisper of His gentle, tender, affectionate, nurturing, unconditional love for each one of us.

Amos the prophet declared himself to be simply a shepherd with a message. I am just that as well. Simply me: wife, momma, cancer survivor, follower of Christ, chief of sinners. I am one who received a Whisper of such great love for me that it now consistently colors everything I see. God's love is victorious. It heals, transforms, equips, and enables us to overcome. It frees us and fills us to love others in truly empowered and fruit-bearing lives. It provides our escape when life's circumstances suffocate us. There *is* a way out of our culture's chaos and our own striving: His name is Jesus.

Believers in Christ are dangerously close to falling asleep in these days, which I believe are the last days. Our hunger for Jesus has lessened—but it *can* be stirred up! The fiery love for Jesus that marked the first-century Christians is possible for us today. The same Spirit in them is in us, ready to produce fruit in us in every season, even our painful ones. Jesus will be returning for us, and where will He find faith? Who is looking to Him? We are, Lord; we are! We will trust. We will look. We will hunger. We will guard quiet space to be with You. We will go out and be Your love. We will pray and never give up (see Luke 18:1). Oh, to be found watchful and working when our King Jesus returns!

The Whisper within equips us to live courageously on the road less traveled. It enables us to bravely circle our Jerichos and refuse the taunts of the enemy as he attempts to make us stop praying, stop loving, stop trying, and stop hoping. The Whisper within reminds us that God's victorious love is more than able to break down any walls of impossibility.

Through private communion with Him, we can become strong in faith, knowing that our Creator is still creating and His voice is still speaking. As the living stones of a holy God, we can stand strong together on God's promises. We can remember that when we go through deep waters, the Lord will be with us (see Isa. 43:2). We can bravely open the doors to hurting places within us, letting the drops of Savior blood heal our hidden wounds. Bursting with the love of God, we can become His messengers, bringing His healing love to satisfy the awaiting sea of thirsty souls around us.

The first part of this book provides six steps that we can take when seeking to hear the Whisper within. The second part shares what His Whisper does—the effect it has on our lives. The ideas in these chapters are by no means exhaustive. Each of us will journey into what fits us. As we seek to live wholly surrendered to our Creator King, we will have our own Holy Spirit experiences.

Each chapter ends with a "Pray It In" section. This was birthed from my realization that every time I have been encouraged by the Word in my prayer closet but leave without "praying the Word in," inevitably within an hour I am left wondering if that special moment actually happened. Some days, the moment I step out of my prayer closet, I am met by my four precious children ready to pounce on me with requests. Taking time to pray it in means spending just a few moments face to the floor, asking God to let His Word and the encouragement it gave us by His Spirit change us, to let it be embedded deeply within us and to protect us from approaching storms in the day ahead through His mighty power at work within us. Each prayer ends with, "Jesus, thank You for taking hold of me today. I rest in Your love."

This book is my cry to those who are weighed down. God's love is the cure for whatever burden we carry. But to grow into the restful, fruitful life God desires for us, we must learn to hear His voice—His written voice, the Bible, and the gentle Whisper of the Spirit's voice within us, illuminating the truth of the Word to our hearts and flooding us with His love. Through the Spirit within me, this book is truly *His* cry to all of us: "Come to me, all of you who are weary and carry heavy burdens, and I will give you rest" (Matt. 11:28).

May it please our heavenly Father to use these pages to spark desire in you for a passionate pursuit of our Creator, the one true God, by spending time with Him in His Word and hearing His Whisper within you. This is my fervent prayer. May your investigation of the Scriptures through the Spirit within you result in a keen awareness of your Creator's vast love for you. He is our tender Father, victorious Savior, and comforting Whisper.

Test everything. Ask Him always. He will manifest Himself to us when we seek Him with our whole hearts (see Jer. 29:13). Luke 11:13 promises that our Father will give us the Spirit when we ask. Keep asking. Keep seeking. Keep knocking. Let us not be shaken, but let us walk fearlessly in these last days as we rest in the calming, equipping, and transforming voice of love: the Whisper within.

IN GRATITUDE

To Momma and Laurie: My "first look" crew! Thank you for the hours you spent combing through the first draft to begin the refining process. Your careful eyes and encouraging hearts are a gift!

To Lauren: The Spirit has gifted you with an exceptional eye for truth and a big heart of love for His people. Your love for Jesus shines brightly to all of us who know you. Thank you for exercising your grace gifts selflessly in the completion of this book.

To Pastor Jerry: Your life speaks of Jesus as King of your heart. He is your living water, a fresh bubbling spring within you spilling over to encourage, comfort, and strengthen the body of Christ (see John 4:14). Thank you for taking precious time to write the foreword for this book. The Spirit in you is powerfully at work to lead God's people in these last days. You were chosen for such a time as this. Your path shines brighter and brighter, Pastor Jerry (see Prov. 4:18)! Soon and very soon.

To Becky: Your capacity to take in an entire manuscript with entire devotion to the truth and love of our Jesus amazes me. You took the message He burned within me to speak and put your whole heart into shaping its clarity. Our heavenly Father knit our friendship together before we were born. You sharpen my awareness of God's love within our conversations and in your pursuit of His kingdom first (see Matt. 6:33). The Spirit in me leaps in joyful recognition of the Spirit in you as we work together with one mind and purpose (see Phil. 2:1–2).

To Rob: Thank you for using your giftings for our Jesus. Your work exceeds even my imagination—and I have a pretty good imagination! This book cover speaks the invitation to come to Jesus and find rest in His love. Your work is beautiful and evidence of a heart that is working for the pleasure of God. Thank you!

To Jennifer: I wish you could have heard how often I said, "That's okay; Jennifer will read this!" as I was trying to comb through the manuscript the final time. Thank you for the time you spent exercising your razor-sharp mind and eyes to bring this book across the finish line.

To my children, Luke, Ellie (Belle), Gracie, and Sammy J: Being your momma has taught me so much about the love of our heavenly Father. You have shown me grace upon grace. From the laughs you bring to the best hugs ever, from making French toast all by yourselves to creating music that stirs the soul, I am blessed beyond measure to have you as my children. May kindness and truth be forever written on your hearts (see Prov. 3:3). Jesus loves you each *so* much! And your momma loves you, forever and ever and always.

To da husband: You have set your sights on the realities of heaven (see Col. 3:1). Your choice to persevere daily strengthens my soul. Thanks for allowing me to stay with my simple pen and paper while you handled the technical side of everything and managed the publishing process of this book. You are a man who follows after Jesus with his whole heart, using his gifts for his King. It is unspeakable joy to be your wife.

To my heavenly Father: I am your fragile jar of clay. You are my great treasure within. Thank You for flooding my heart with Your love, for responding with great faithfulness to my earnest asking to understand more about this unbreakable love that You have for me. Only You can open the eyes of hearts. Please, Father, take these pages that fall so short and speak Your love to Your people. I am so glad I am Your forever girl. I love You, Abba.

PART 1

PREPARING *to* HEAR

1

CREATING
QUIET SPACES

Relishing the quietness of the early August morning, I climbed into my car to begin a one-hour drive to a Christian women's conference. Night lingered in the summer skies, pulling my gaze up to the sea of stars twinkling above the massive Southern California mountains. The beauty drew my thoughts to the One who had spoken it into existence: my Creator. One God. Father, Son, and Holy Spirit. The familiar prayer came again: "Teach me, Lord. Teach me more about Your love. About Your rest. About Yourself as my good Father."

I began praying aloud. The passenger seats were empty, but the car suddenly felt full. It was me with my Father, who was manifesting Himself to me in response to my asking. What followed was a spiritual encounter that changed me for eternity: I sobbed in quiet wonder as the still small Whisper within me whispered three times, "*I love you. I love you. I love you.*"

"Father?"

"*Yes, it's Me.*" Then it came again into the innermost place of my being: "*I love you. I love you. I love you.*"

"*Yes, My daughter. I love you with an unbreakable love. I have loved you this way your whole life. Your performance didn't start My love, and your mistakes can't stop it. Your worth is determined by one thing: My love for you.*"

I melted in a flood of tears at this precious word from my Father. For most of my life, my love for God had been centered on trying to make Him happy and trying to make people happy. All this self-effort had led to overwork. Add to that the non-Hodgkin's lymphoma diagnosis I'd received several years earlier with all its fear and conflicting advice and treatments and side effects, along with the daily juggling that came with homeschooling four children, and my heart had become heavy and tired.

"*May I enter those places of hurt in you tucked away from human vision? I see them. And I see you. My tender Father love breathes healing into your wounds. It will wash away guilt, disappointments, and regrets that are weighing down your soul.*"

Besides the exhaustion I felt, I carried a constant awareness of my inadequacies. Trying to please God all the time couldn't help but lead to disappointment in myself! The Lord gently began to show me that my self-effort was not the way to please Him; instead, *He* was the One who would work in me the desire and the power to do what pleased Him (see Phil. 2:13). My job was to relax in His love; He would bring about the fruit in my life that He desired and that would bring me peace.

"*When your heart grows tired, come to Me. Rest in My love. Your resting will lead to your doing, and the work you do then will be Me working through you, not you striving. You will love others because I first loved you. You will step into My life, My Word, My Spirit. It will be overflow, not overwork. It will be slow, not hurried. It will be peace, not unrest. Daughter, My love for you is not about what you do; it's about who I AM.*"

This encounter gave me a new and deep awareness of the vastness of God's love for me. His love entered into every painful crevice of my soul, bringing His healing and a fresh filling of His Spirit unlike anything I had yet experienced.

Ephesians 5:18 gives the command, *"Be filled* with the Holy Spirit." Of course, all who have given their hearts to Jesus have been baptized into one body by one Spirit, so the Spirit *is* living in us (see 1 Cor. 12:13)—the Holy Spirit has been residing in me since I gave my heart to Jesus at the tender age of five! But as I became more aware of my Father's love for me, my awareness of the Holy Spirit's presence with me and my earnest desire for His control over me increased.

Though I had grown up singing "Jesus loves me, this I know," it was on August 25, 2018, that I experienced His love racing throughout my being in response to my earnest asking. It was similar to when I look into the eyes of my young children and say, "I love you!" and radiance lights up their precious faces. I lost *me* in the overwhelming wave of my Creator's love, and there I found the deepest peace.

TIME TO GET QUIET

Five months of the Spirit's prompting me to pray for revival preceded my encounter with God in the car that summer day. It had started in March 2018, as a deepening hunger for God consumed me. I was grieved by all the smartphones blocking my view of faces around me at stores, libraries, parks, restaurants, neighborhood sidewalks—even my mountain hiking paths.

The screen intrudes on quiet spaces, steals time for conversations, blocks us from noticing needs—and fills margins in our day meant for connecting with God. An ache for change gnawed at my insides. Despite the time I spent regularly reading the Bible, praying, and gathering with local believers at church, something was missing. This ache sparked in me daily prayer for revival.

After several weeks of seeking the Lord for revival, our Father gently instructed me that revival starts with me and invited me to something more: a forty-day feast with Him. Anticipation met me each morning as I woke and thought of my noon appointment to dine with Jesus, feasting on His Word at my mountain bench three miles from our California home. This practice of a scriptural meal once a day during my forty-day feast sensitized my ear to God's gentle voice within me, preparing my heart to better hear His Whisper of love.

Two years have passed since that morning the Father powerfully manifested His love to me through the Whisper within—three Whispers from the three coequal Persons of the Trinity. While I have never heard the audible voice of God, as I have continued to deepen my communion with Jesus, He has increased my recognition of His clear, quiet voice within me.

Our Creator designed our souls to rest in Him. We can see this as we gaze upon the birds that He cares for and remember that our value is greater than that of a sparrow (see Matt. 10:31). As we study the movement of clouds, we can recognize God's Spirit moving purposefully within us in the same way. Much as the ocean tide comes in and out in divine rhythm, we were created for rhythms of rest built into our days. Some mornings I giggle with my youngest child, Sammy J, as we watch the chipmunks playing tag along the top of our backyard fence and talk about God's creativity on display as the squirrels chatter. God's smile grows with ours when we take time to stop, look, and listen for His truth.

It is in quiet rest that our work becomes fruitful. Being still helps us make the switch from self to Spirit as the force moving throughout our days. We must learn to protect time alone with our Father, or the waters of our inner beings will slowly dry up. Time spent with our living water, Jesus, will revive our souls. With our whole beings, body and soul, we will shout joyfully to the living God (see Ps. 84:2).

CREATING QUIET SPACES BEGINS WITH PRAYER

Change *is* possible. We can learn to stop listening to all the voices around us and within us and start listening for the Holy Spirit's Whisper within. But change starts with prayer. The Spirit begins to shape us from within when we pray.

Daily fervent prayer without ceasing, however, begins only when we commit to creating quiet spaces. We must make quiet spaces for prayer, and we must also practice pausing *during* our prayer times. Then the silent spaces will begin to be filled by the voice of the Spirit within us. He will lead us by still waters, increasing our hunger to keep calm hearts so we can then move with untroubled souls into the busier parts of our days.

Seeking to cut back on the clutter that fills our minds, schedules, and living spaces is an excellent first step for enlarging quiet spaces in our lives. It helps to designate a special spot where we can go to meet with God. My kids know that my chosen spots here in the Northwest, where we returned in May 2019 after two years in California, are my prayer closet and the nature park by our home. The habit of meeting with God each morning in my quiet space feeds my hunger to maintain my interaction with Him as I transition into the noise of my day.

Creating quiet spaces takes intentionality. I have found six ways to be helpful in planning time to be still with my Creator.

GUARDING MORNING COMMUNION

Brilliant colors grew in the morning sky over the California mountains dressed in spring. Birds chattered cheerfully. Tucking my coat around me a bit more tightly, I breathed in the cool promising air of the day ahead. I pulled out my little pink notebook and turned the worn pages back one year to March 2018—where the word "revival" first began to pop up on every page. Scanning my barely legible writing, I traveled through my forty days of daily feasting with Jesus before my eyes stopped. Yes, there it was, August 25, 2018: "*I love you. I love you. I love you.*" Three times.

I turned the pages ahead to September 12, 2018, the day when this book, *The Whisper Within*, was birthed in my heart before morning's light. The Lord had awakened me at four thirty that morning, when I was alone in a hotel room, drawing me into delightful, powerful communion with Him. The Whisper within came minutes after my sleepy self had sat up in bed: "*Feed My sheep.*"

"Me, Lord? How?"

"*Write. Write about My love—My shepherd's heart that carries My lambs tenderly, loving and nurturing each one with My unconditional love. Write through the lens of My Spirit within you who sees in people's eyes their untold stories—stories of unhealed wounds, tired hearts, and wearied minds. Write about how I whispered My love to you in the car on August 25, 2018, speaking to you as your Papa, your Beloved, your Whisper. Tell everyone of My love and My longing for them.*"

Drawing my awareness back to the birds singing happily around me on this quiet Sunday morning, I closed my little pink book. My smile stretched wide as I sunk a bit deeper into the love of our triune God, a mystery I have yet to fully grasp and that wraps my soul in wonder. Looking up once more into the lingering pink hues of the Sunday sunrise, I stood up from my bench. I was ready to make the short three-mile drive home to my waiting family, hug them tightly, and move through this new day aware of the peaceful presence of the Spirit within me.

Jesus set the example for us to follow when He walked the earth. He went to solitary places to pray long before daylight.

My best communion time is when I am alone in the quiet hours of the morning. When we lived in Southern California, that mountain bench was one of two quiet spaces where I communed with God. The other was my prayer closet, where I went more regularly.

My children, Luke, Ellie, Gracie, and Sammy J, are now twelve, ten, eight, and seven and have recognized that Momma is kinder if she has been in her prayer closet. They sometimes run in to give me a picture, brush my hair, or hug me and say, "Have a good prayer time!" Every so often Steve stands guard if it has been an exceptionally difficult week. He sees the change in me after Jesus has had a say in my day. I laughed hard when I heard a Christian comedian on the radio say that his job when his wife was having her quiet time with Jesus became running after the four- and six-year-olds, shouting, "Don't bother Momma!" Yup, that sounds like Steve!

Even after years of me heading into my closet early in the mornings, we still have days every so often that go south. The mornings tend to be bumpy after holidays, family visits, and trips as we find our way back into routines.

I held high hopes in my heart on our first day back to regular routines in a new year and a new decade as I fell asleep the first Sunday night of January in 2020. Steve and I had set an alarm for five thirty. He planned to take Luke, our oldest, out for a special breakfast. I planned to spend a long time with Jesus before getting breakfast together at home for the younger three. I was ready for a smooth return to our homeschool routines.

By six I was a frustrated mess of tears. If only my kids had an internal clock that I could program for them to wake up at seven! All three younger kids were up, squabbling and needing me for this and that. I wish I could tell you that I handled it with grace. Sigh.

But my mess-ups increase my gratitude for the grace of our Jesus that never runs dry. It's like when my dad took me golfing in my younger years; when I missed the ball completely, he sometimes gave me a mulligan and let me try again. Sometimes I have to take a mulligan with my kids. We collapse in a heap of tears, share a hug, and try again.

As I sighed in exasperation over the fact that I needed a mulligan so soon in the new year, I noticed the drooping houseplant on the mantle that I had once again forgotten to water. I carried the plant upstairs to my prayer closet and invited in my three remorseful children, each looking a bit unsure about this invitation into grumpy Momma's prayer closet.

"This is what I wake up like each day, dear Ellie, Gracie, and Sammy J," I told them. We sat a minute on my closet floor observing the sad-looking plant. Then I gave Ellie a glass of water, explaining to the children that the water was like Jesus, His Word, and His Spirit. When we squabble before the sun rises, Momma is like a droopy plant without energy for the day. When Momma has some quiet time in the early mornings with Jesus, she is like a happy plant.

Ellie poured water on the plant, which perked up as the day went along. We took time to notice how much happier it looked by the afternoon, remembering that we all are like plants, divinely designed to be green and full of life. God has countless mulligans available to us and is honored by our repeated returns to Him.

Feasting with God causes the worries we wake up with to dissipate. Practicing the daily discipline of private communion with Jesus also feeds our desire for increased time with Him. Joy rises up as we become aware of the Spirit's presence in us.

When we guard morning communion times before gathering with other believers, our hearts become tuned to the Spirit, granting us a deeper awareness of His presence within us. This will feed our passion to spread an awareness of His love everywhere He takes us. Our time together with others will be deeper and sweeter to our souls because of the time we have spent alone with God.

Minimizing Interruptions

Devices threaten to steal our attentiveness to God and to one another. One discipline that can increase the quiet recharge moments in our days is putting away or turning off our smartphones for certain periods of time. It can help to have a dedicated time of day focused on sending phone messages for prayer and encouragement to others and then putting our phones away in a place where we will not be distracted by them.

We can also choose to put smartphones away when we gather with others. Without the distraction of our rectangular companions, we are better able to listen to people with our eyes, ears, and hearts. We send the message to them, "You are important. I value our time together. You matter to me."

We can visualize this particularly in the sacred dwelling place for God that forms when we gather with other believers for church. As a church body, we become the temple that He fills. We can minimize potential distractions and interruptions, for ourselves and for others, by using a paper Bible during the sermon rather than a smartphone. What joy rises when a crowd of believers, all filled with the Spirit and focused on Him, praise the Lord with one voice!

Periodically choosing silence in the car over the radio can gift us moments of quiet when traveling to appointments or gatherings. Songs on the radio *can* be encouraging, of course. I love to worship while I drive. The kids giggle when I can't help but sing or raise my hand in response to a song. One day I glanced in the rearview mirror to see both Gracie and Sammy J singing in the backseat with lifted hands. Some days, though, we can use this time for quiet rather than music in order to tune in to our Father and enjoy His presence.

Committing to Lighter Schedules

Sometimes we just need to simplify—to empty our calendars. A life reset will benefit us, our marriages, and our families. Galatians 5 teaches us that we should not be under slavery to people but instead are to be led of the Spirit. One way to put this truth into practice is to ask the Spirit to lead us in every commitment we add to our calendars.

In some seasons the Lord not only equips us but also *calls* us to more commitments. This will always be part of the good that He planned for us to do before we were born (see Eph. 2:10). In other seasons circumstances will call for lighter schedules. One way to know if our calendars need some lightening is what I call the "blanket test": when you look at your calendar, does a sudden urge overtake you to run to your room and throw a blanket over your head and hide? In seasons of great affliction, it is important that we have light schedules so our quiet spaces can remain quiet spaces.

Letting the Spirit control everything we do is the answer. Creating margin in our days allows us to guard our communion with Jesus and avoid checking our devices until after our morning time with Him. Implementing a "margin for honor" also allows us time for honoring those unexpected encounters with hurting hearts that God may bring our way. A longing to spread the good news of Jesus and His love should be the greatest factor influencing our yeses and no's to commitments.

Engaging in Relationships Through Prayer

Jesus loved all people. But He had an inner three and a group of disciples with whom He spent more time (see Matt. 17:1). Jesus spent all night praying before He selected the twelve disciples (see Luke 6:12–16). In the same way, prayer should precede our decisions as to whom we spend time with. We become like the people we draw near. When we try to meet with too many people, our schedules crowd out the *One* with whom we should meet first and most.

It is hard not to say yes to every opportunity to meet with others, but saying no is vital to maintaining healthy souls. Not a single one of us can do everything for everyone. But all of us can be used by the Lord to meet some needs. The secret is to pray first and then obey. The Lord always equips for any relationships to which He calls us. Always!

Making Room for Meditation

Andrew Murray describes the Spirit-filled life as an "intense, close, personal attachment to Jesus and fellowship with Him every day."[1] Murray made a habit of creating quiet spaces for times of prayer and meditation to "receive lessons from God."[2] He spent time listening for God to teach him about all that he had taken in through his senses after traveling around to the homes and farms of the people in his congregation. This gave me pause as I thought of how often I move from activity to activity without taking time to ponder what I have seen and heard, asking God to change me to become more like Him through my spiritual encounters and conversations.

When we consider those who have gone before us who were Spirit filled, we see the role that quiet spaces had in growing their fervor for God. Andrew Murray was one, but there are countless others. A. W. Tozer is another favorite of mine. He wrote, "Come near to the holy men and women of the past and you will soon feel the heat of their desire after God. They mourned for Him, they prayed and wrestled and sought for Him day and night, in season and out, and when they found Him the finding was all the sweeter for the long seeking."[3]

Making room for meditation is an important step in creating quiet spaces throughout our days. Even five minutes has an impact. I love to go to my room in the evenings and lie down on my bedroom floor for five minutes, placing my arms out as if I was on the cross where Jesus was, to thank, praise, ask, and listen. This leads to the last step of the day: the evening return.

RETURNING TO RHYTHMIC REST

When God created the heavens and the earth, it says that "evening passed and morning came, marking the first day" (Gen. 1:5). God created us as beings who crave rhythm in our days. Carving out time in the evenings for rest helps us return to quiet spaces with God as we finish each day.

God created not just daily rhythm but also weekly: "On the seventh day God had finished his work of creation, so he rested from all his work" (Gen. 2:2). When we get to the seventh day, we can follow the rhythm God intended for us as His chosen created beings to display His glory: we were made to stop working at the end of the week and have a day when we simply stop to rest, to enter into deeper worship.

God designed us to be recharged by Him, but the hurry in our world doesn't sleep. We must choose rest. A couple years ago I started turning my phone off on the weekends to give my mind a chance to truly turn off and renew. I was surprised by the wave of peace and calm that settled in my soul. I felt free. My brain was completely available to think on God, to look up into the sky and take in His handiwork.

For my always-thinking mind, the transition from phone on to phone off was like standing in New York City as all businesses shut down for the day, all public transportation suddenly ceased, and quietness blanketed the city that never sleeps. Limiting the noise coming in helps us connect with the Person who lives within His people and longs for our full attention.

A farmer's land is more productive when it is given a season to rest. The same is true with the soil of our hearts. When we practice regular rest days, we are filled with soul nutrition from hearing God's voice and being in His Word. To skip the Sabbath is to function in a state of chronic depletion. Our whole beings are renewed for the new day and new week ahead when we practice an evening return and a weekly Sabbath.

As we create quiet spaces and begin to continually hear the Spirit's Whisper within telling us of His love, it will change how we spend our moments. His love will spill out from us to those in our spheres of influence. Our broken human love doesn't change lives, but the holy, healing love of our Creator overflowing from His Spirit within us does. We love each other because He first loved us (see 1 John 4:19). He clothes us with kindness, compassion, gentleness, humility, and patience (see Col. 3:12). We were created to live lives filled with love (see Eph. 5:2). When we walk in step with His Whisper within us, resting in the perfect love He has for us, the result is not just good news for us but also good news for *others*. Paul speaks of this being the good news that changes lives! How is our time with Jesus changing our hearts toward others today (see Col. 1:8)?

As we engage in personal pursuit of Jesus, may the peace and stillness of Christ in us help us open our hands in complete surrender—the posture of an untroubled heart. When we create quiet spaces, we will awaken to His presence and receive moment by moment His tender, nurturing, and restful love.

✢ *Pray It In* ✢

Father, still the treadmill of my thoughts as I spend time in the pages of Your written voice listening to the voice of Your Spirit teach and comfort me. Your instructions revive my soul. Your words bring joy to my heart and light to my eyes. Your words, oh Lord, are more desirable than gold, sweeter than honey. They are a warning to me and a great reward when I obey them (see Ps. 19:8, 10–11).

Jesus, thank You for taking hold of me today. I rest in Your love.

2

RETURNING TO
REVERENCE

Clouds capture my attention. All shapes, sizes, and colors dress the skies over my Northwest home. Observing the clouds stirs up joyful anticipation in me of our Beloved's nearing return (see Luke 21:27)! It also makes me think of Jesus' first coming, when His very feet walked this earth two thousand years ago, and His eyes scanned the skies too! I wonder what clouds He saw when He looked up before breaking the bread that fed the five thousand. I don't know, but I do see in Jesus' example that He took time for holy silence, to look up and connect with His Father, to focus on His powerful presence.

Looking up makes us aware of God. This should lead us to reverent thankfulness. Looking up creates an opportunity for us to pause and remember who God is and where our help comes from (see Ps. 121:2). It helps us listen less to the voices around us that point out every flaw within us and our relationships that need to be fixed. It raises our eyes from our current circumstances, bringing into view the One whose voice holds authority over all things.

Looking up daily will train our minds to think first on God. Focusing our thoughts on God enthrones Jesus as the King of our hearts who rules our thoughts, attitudes, and actions. As we look up, we begin to properly revere Him as the author of all who is present with us now, listening to us, and willing and able to help us. He is a good Father, giving rest to His loved ones (see Ps. 127:2).

Not a single gifting, positive thought, or blessing is present in our lives that was not given to us by our Father who longs to bless us. He is infinitely creative in His dealings with His children. Think about Jonah and how God's rescue came in the form of a huge fish! God allowed Jonah to spend three long days in the stinky belly of the fish. I cannot wait to ask Jonah about this experience! God could have wiped Jonah out for his disobedience of not going to Nineveh as He had asked. The story of Jonah reminds me of God's rich mercy and power over all creation. Even the big fish obey His voice. No circumstance is bigger than our God. Bowing before Him in humble adoration, we raise the eyes of our soul to gaze upon our risen Savior, who victoriously rains down new life, new mercies, new strength, and new grace for our days, calming our troubled souls.

Into this sacred place of reverence comes the grandest blessing of all: we realize that this mighty God lives in us through His Holy Spirit. When reverence of God meets this reality of His presence in us, peace reigns. Peace louder than trial. Peace wiping clean the lies that darken our soul. Peace present despite unsolved mysteries. Peace that comes from knowing His voice silencing the storm. "God is greatly to be feared in the assembly of the saints, and to be held in reverence by all those around Him. O LORD God of hosts, who is mighty like You, O LORD? Your faithfulness also surrounds You. You rule the raging of the sea; when its waves rise, You still them" (Ps. 89:7–9, NKJV).

REMOVING OUR SHOES

Moses was going about his daily grind, caring for his father-in-law's flock, when he took note of a bush on fire that didn't seem to be burning up. As he walked over to get a closer look, "God called to him out of the bush, 'Moses, Moses!' And he said, 'Here I am.' Then he said, 'Do not come near; take your sandals off your feet, for the place on which you are standing is holy ground.' And he said, 'I am the God of your father, the God of Abraham, the God of Isaac, and the God of Jacob.' And Moses hid his face, for he was afraid to look at God" (Exod. 3:4–6, ESV). Moses was overwhelmed by God's holiness. He removed his shoes in obedience and in recognition of the holy ground he was about to walk on.

Joshua had his own experience on holy ground after he took over as leader of the Israelites. He was standing near Jericho when suddenly a man stood in front of him holding a sword. When Joshua questioned whether he was friend or foe, the man responded, "Neither one. . . . I am the commander of the LORD's army" (Josh. 5:14). Joshua's response was to fall to the ground in reverence, asking the commander what his marching orders were. The commander told him, " 'Take off your sandals, for the place where you are standing is holy.' And Joshua did as he was told" (Josh. 5:15).

I spent the first few years of my childhood as a missionary kid in Japan, where it was customary for people to remove their shoes before entering others' homes to protect the floors from the dirt and grime of the streets. When we meet with God, the idea of removing our shoes represents our recognition of His position as God and our position as His creation. We leave pride at the door to enter His sanctuary. We bow before Him, worshiping the great I AM, Creator and Sustainer of all. He alone is worthy of all glory, honor, and praise. When we "take off our shoes," we come empty-handed and barefoot to our Creator, ready for His teaching.

When we mentally remove our shoes, we find our "why" questions disappearing into the beauty of who He is, praising Him instead of running down a list of "Please do this for me, God." Our "asks" become an overflow of praise:

Let all that I am praise the LORD.
O LORD my God, how great you are! You are robed with honor and majesty. You are dressed in a robe of light. You stretch out the starry curtain of the heavens; you lay out the rafters of your home in the rain clouds. You make the clouds your chariot; you ride upon the wings of the wind. The winds are your messengers; flames of fire are your servants.
You placed the world on its foundation so it would never be moved. (Ps. 104:1–5)

Fear of God can be thought of as reverent awe. Without reverent awe, we forget that prayer is sacred, and we tend to be quick to speak, slow to listen, and quite expressive of our opinions. Reverent awe returns our attention to promise after promise that is ours in Jesus.

With shoes removed, we stand firm on Christ the solid rock. As we begin to reverence His presence, He fills us with trust as we wait on Him. Our confidence in Him grows as we choose praise (see Ps. 108:1). We stop trusting our own thoughts, trading them for His Spirit's voice of truth within us. We hope in His mercy alone, knowing that His gaze is upon us as daughters and sons of God. He fashions our hearts individually and considers our works (see Ps. 33:13–15). The eye of the Lord is on those who fear Him, on those who hope in His mercy (see Ps. 33:18). The *God* of the universe *sees* us! From His throne over all, He *bends* His ear down to listen to us (see Ps. 116:2)!

Grasping the truth that He rules over all changes how we pray, how we wait, and how we trust. Moses and Aaron were given a consequence for not trusting and obeying God's command. The people wanted water, and Moses was told to *speak* to the rock, and water would come out. But he whacked the rock twice instead of speaking and awaiting God's movement. As a result, he did not get to enter the promised land.

Oh, how many times have we whacked instead of waited? How often has God said, "Speak," and instead of obeying Him and waiting for Him to move we have tried to do things our own way? I grieve the days when my lack of total trust in God has blocked me from experiencing the fruit-filled life that Jesus longs to give. Reverent awe encourages this kind of trust. Remembering who God is helps us release what our fists have closed around.

PONDERING OUR TRIUNE GOD

I shake my head in wonder at how patient God has been with me despite my stark similarities to the Israelites. Moses was a man of God and yet made mistakes. But we hold the power of choice: we can focus on our mess-ups or remember our deliverer. Nehemiah 9 is an excellent passage to help us pause and ponder the character of God. These six verses below, in particular, have returned me to reverent awe of God in times when I have been drifting into too much "me" and not enough "Him":

> They and our fathers acted presumptuously and stiffened their neck and did not obey your commandments. They refused to obey and were not mindful of the wonders that you performed among them, but they stiffened their neck and appointed a leader to return to their slavery in Egypt. But you are a God ready to forgive, gracious and merciful, slow to anger and abounding in steadfast love, and did not forsake them. Even when they had made for themselves a golden calf and said, "This is your God who brought you up out of Egypt," and had committed great blasphemies,

you in your great mercies did not forsake them in the wilderness. The pillar of cloud to lead them in the way did not depart from them by day, nor the pillar of fire by night to light for them the way by which they should go. You gave your good Spirit to instruct them and did not withhold your manna from their mouth and gave them water for their thirst. Forty years you sustained them in the wilderness, and they lacked nothing. Their clothes did not wear out and their feet did not swell. (Neh. 9:16–21, ESV)

God our Father sent His very Word, His only Son, to rescue us. Jesus came to do the precise will of the Father, to speak His words. Then when Jesus rose up to heaven, He promised us that the Father would send His very Spirit (see John 14:26).

There is a mesmerizing, unbreakable circle of love and oneness flowing within the Trinity of Father-Son-Spirit. Taking time each day to ponder the Trinity increases reverent awe of Him. To think about each Person in our one God is to explore an infinite ocean of the purest love. It is helpful to speak this truth when lies grow loud: "Through Christ in me, I confidently hope in God's mercy. I will think upon this triune God on whom I wait. He sees me. He hears me. I am His personal concern. He is my very present help."

Remembering God's Absolute Authority

After almost two years without a migraine, one recently whirled in on me fast and furious, debilitating my body and discouraging my soul. I reached out to a couple of friends for prayer. One of the responses that came back from a pastor friend included a passage he had been studying in Isaiah 45. With that the Lord put a big stop sign in front of my "Dr. Google" Q&A session on hormonal migraines and a green light to search Isaiah 45 instead. The

Whisper came from within, *"There is a goldmine here for you today, My daughter!"*

When my head pain decreased enough for me to manage reading, I combed through Isaiah 45 over and over again. The fruit kept falling from the prospering Word of God, nourishing my soul, which had grown lean under the longevity of chronic health issues. Isaiah 45 brought me back to a place of reverence for God rather than one of questioning my Creator.

Isaiah 45:9 states, "What sorrow awaits those who argue with their Creator. Does a clay pot argue with its maker? Does the clay dispute with the one who shapes it, saying, 'Stop, you're doing it wrong!'" My Father reminded me in Isaiah 45:5–7, "I am the LORD. There is no other God. I have equipped you for battle, though you don't even know me, so all the world from east to west will know there is no other God. I am the LORD, and there is no other. I create the light and make the darkness. I send good times and bad times. I, the LORD, am the one who does these things.'"

This dear friend fed my soul through sharing what God was teaching him during his own valley season. Romans 8:28 had also been strongly impressed on his heart after reading Isaiah 45. We will experience hard times, but it is ultimately all for our good and kingdom growth.

When we lose strong reverence for our Creator, we start to elevate how we think our lives should go rather than live out of worship to the One who knows exactly what He is doing. "This is what the LORD says—the Holy One of Israel and your Creator: 'Do you question what I do for my children? Do you give me orders about the work of my hands? I am the one who made the earth and created people to live on it. With my hands I stretched out the heavens. All the stars are at my command'" (Isa. 45:11–12). On this eternal Word we must stand. We should take God at His Word, resolving to not be swayed, even when, as Danny Gokey sings, "I just haven't seen it yet."[1]

Faith is believing what we cannot see. When we return to reverence, we remember that our Creator sees eternity but that our own sight is incomplete: "Now we see things imperfectly, like puzzling reflections in a mirror, but then we will see everything with perfect clarity. All that I know now is partial and incomplete, but then I will know everything completely, just as God now knows me completely" (1 Cor. 13:12).

God speaks in both light and darkness, faithfully answering the cries of His children for help. We read one example of this in Daniel 2:17–23. Daniel called out to God for help when King Nebuchadnezzar sent out a decree for all the wise men of Babylon to be killed for not being able to interpret the king's dream:

> Daniel went home and told his friends Hananiah, Mishael, and Azariah what had happened. He urged them to ask the God of heaven to show them his mercy by telling them the secret, so they would not be executed along with the other wise men of Babylon. That night the secret was revealed to Daniel in a vision. Then Daniel praised the God of heaven. He said, "Praise the name of God forever and ever, for he has all wisdom and power. He controls the course of world events; he removes kings and sets up other kings. He gives wisdom to the wise and knowledge to the scholars. He reveals deep and mysterious things and knows what lies hidden in darkness, though he is surrounded by light. I thank and praise you, God of my ancestors, for you have given me wisdom and strength. You have told me what we asked of you and revealed to us what the king demanded."

Daniel didn't fly solo. He got his three close friends together to seek God's face—to plead for help because of God's mercy. Jesus had His inner three too! It is good to seek intercessors when clouds form overhead. Daniel also made sure to give glory to its proper

Owner when he reported to King Nebuchadnezzar the meaning of the dream: "There are no wise men, enchanters, magicians, or fortune-tellers who can reveal the king's secret. But there is a God in heaven who reveals secrets, and he has shown King Nebuchadnezzar what will happen in the future. Now I will tell you your dream and the visions you saw as you lay on your bed" (Dan. 2:27–28).

Scripture holds countless reminders that God holds authority over all circumstances. After Samuel gave Eli the prophecy he had received about events to come in Eli's life, Eli's response was, "It is the LORD. Let Him do what seems good to Him" (1 Sam. 3:18, NKJV). Eli recognized the sovereignty of God over all things. God is the great I AM, who also happens to love having His children curl up against Him in trust that He is working all things for kingdom good.

PRAYING THE WORD

Oh, to cry out to our Father, to be reverent in our approach to His Word, protected from picking it up in a casual way and remembering that it is the divinely inspired Word of our living God! Oh, to tremble at the power and authority indelibly etched into every letter of Scripture. Jesus was the Word, and the Word was with God, and the Word was God (see John 1:1). The Word has all authority over our lives.

At times we may not know how to pray. During such moments I cry out, "Spirit, pray through me!" I open my Bible, often to the book of Psalms, and begin to pray the Word. We can pray God's written voice over our hearts, minds, bodies, and souls. We can pray it over our families, friends, cities, countries, and the world. We can pray it over the lost, the broken, the oppressed, and those in despair. It is the sword of the Spirit, and there is no better way to fight than with the Word of God—for then *God* is fighting for us.

Here are some of my favorite weapons of war:

By awesome deeds in righteousness You will answer us, O God of our salvation, You who are the confidence of all the ends of the earth, and of the far-off seas; who established the mountains by His strength, being clothed with power; You who still the noise of the seas, the noise of their waves, and the tumult of the peoples. (Ps. 65:5–7, NKJV)

Powerful is your arm! Strong is your hand! Your right hand is lifted high in glorious strength! (Ps. 89:13)

Ascribe strength to God; His excellence is over Israel, and His strength is in the clouds. O God, You are more awesome than Your holy places. The God of Israel is He who gives strength and power to His people. Blessed be God! (Ps. 68:34–35, NKJV)

Numerous times since I was diagnosed with cancer at Christmas in 2013, God's Word has been my victory. In my darkest hours, speaking the name of Jesus into my room, singing hymns such as "It Is Well with My Soul," and reading Scripture aloud have rescued me from the tempest of my thoughts, bringing me into a place of peace-filled victory.

IS JESUS ENOUGH?

Sometimes we are in seasons of waiting. Prayers seem to go unanswered. Scripture teaches that all God's creation waits for their Creator to work on their behalf. "They all depend on you to give them food as they need it. When you supply it, they gather it. You open your hand to feed them, and they are richly satisfied" (Ps. 104:27–28).

In one season of fervent intercession that extended day after day without the movement of God that I was hoping for, a question from the Lord rose up in my soul: *Am I enough for you?*"

Oh, the quieting that came over me as this powerful Whisper came from within. Was it true? Was Jesus enough? Contemplating the beauty, truth, and value of Jesus my Savior, the Spirit pointed me to Psalm 84 and a time of tearful meditation. Peace held me once again. "Yes, Jesus, You are enough!" What an anchor to the soul!

How lovely is your dwelling place, O LORD of Heaven's Armies. I long, yes, I faint with longing to enter the courts of the LORD. With my whole being, body and soul, I will shout joyfully to the living God. Even the sparrow finds a home, and the swallow builds her nest and raises her young at a place near your altar, O LORD of Heaven's Armies, my King and my God! What joy for those who can live in your house, always singing your praises. *Interlude*

What joy for those whose strength comes from the LORD, who have set their minds on a pilgrimage to Jerusalem. When they walk through the Valley of Weeping, it will become a place of refreshing springs. The autumn rains will clothe it with blessings. They will continue to grow stronger, and each of them will appear before God in Jerusalem.

O LORD God of Heaven's Armies, hear my prayer. Listen, O God of Jacob. *Interlude*

O God, look with favor upon the king, our shield! Show favor to the one you have anointed.

A single day in your courts is better than a thousand anywhere else! I would rather be a gatekeeper in the house of my God than live the good life in the homes of the wicked. For the LORD God is our sun and our shield. He gives us grace and glory. The LORD will withhold no good thing from those who do what is right. O LORD of Heaven's Armies, what joy for those who trust in you. (Ps. 84)

When we return to reverence, we assume an expectant waiting position, recognizing God as authority over every part of our minds, bodies, souls, relationships, and circumstances. We trust in His absolute power to act on our behalf in His perfectly timed moment. Waiting on Him "combines the deep sense of our entire helplessness to work what is divinely good, and our perfect confidence that God will work it all by His divine power."[2] We sense His powerful, calming presence within us as we wait, resting with childlike trust in our Creator's enduring love.

⸺ *Pray It In* ⸺

Adonai, my Lord, how excellent is Your name over all the earth (see Ps. 8:1)! "You are the LORD, you alone. You have made heaven, the heaven of heavens, with all their host, the earth and all that is on it, the seas and all that is in them; and you preserve all of them; and the host of heaven worships you" (Neh. 9:6, ESV). You gather the wind in the palm of Your hand (see Prov. 30:4). Oh, how great are Your riches and wisdom and knowledge! How impossible it is for me to understand Your decisions and Your ways (see Rom. 11:33)! I remain thankful, Father, worshiping You with holy fear and awe (see Heb. 12:28).

Jesus, thank You for taking hold of me today. I rest in Your love.

3

THE ISAAC ALTAR

My shoulders excel in the art of tension trapping. Stress makes its home there as a physical manifestation of an inward condition when I slip into "fix it myself" mode. I crumble under weights that I was not created to carry. It starts subtly and then expands into crushing despair that settles deep into my bones. A pastor's wife once helped me with this by sharing with me the meaning of Exodus 14:14: "The LORD will fight for you; you need only to be still" (NIV). She said to be still meant to let my arms hang down. It was a picture of total surrender.

I visualize total surrender with what I call the Isaac altar. When I step into the same moment of truth that Abraham did when God asked him to lay his only son on the altar (see Gen. 22:1–18), I am faced with identical questions: Do I love God most? Is *He* alone enough? Is He enough when a migraine pierces my head and awakens me in the middle of the night? Is He enough when my cancer test results aren't what I hoped for? Is He enough when one of my children is struggling—again? Is He enough when another day goes by without the answer to that same prayer I've been praying for decades? Is Jesus enough for me?

When I let my arms hang the first time, it surprised me how much tension I had been carrying between my shoulders. When life grows overwhelming, breathing in deeply and letting our arms hang as we exhale opens us up to receive peace, hope, and quiet joy. We can bravely open the doors of our hearts for God's searchlight to show us who or what we have started to hold onto—and how we need to put it on the Isaac altar. We can join David's prayer, "Search me, O God, and know my heart; test me and know my anxious thoughts. Point out anything in me that offends you, and lead me along the path of everlasting life" (Ps. 139:23–24).

As we let our arms hang, dropping our shoulders and emptying our hands, the Spirit gently begins to sweep clean little un-surrendered pockets in our souls. His love and light flood the darkened corners and replace chaos with His peaceful rule as King of our hearts. When we surrender completely, our concerns are quieted as He gently folds us into all of Him. The Father longs to draw His children into Himself, wanting us to know that He alone is able to provide for all needs at all times.

Our daily full surrender enables our troubled souls to be calmed by the voice of our Savior. We can pray, "Adonai, You are my Shepherd; I have all that I need. You let me rest in green meadows; You lead me next to still waters. You restore my soul. You calm my mind and my heart, and You shape my desires. You guide me along right paths for the sake of Your kingdom" (see Ps. 23:1–3; 103:1).

The Isaac altar makes us aware of when we are elevating anything or anyone above God and His desires. When we can squeak out our broken hallelujahs, "Father, You *are enough*," He rushes to meet us, His trembling children. His presence swoops in to bear us up and hold us tight. He removes the weights crushing us. We can lose ourselves in His strong arms, receiving everything that He desires to be for us: peace, hope, and joy; mercies new, morning by morning; grace that delivers; grace that sustains; hope not defined by past experiences; hope that stays after the rainbow fades.

As we enter heaven's waiting room, that place of waiting at the Savior's feet, we find that we are not alone. Many others are waiting too. God sees this trust of His waiting children who have let go of their very dearest possession upon their Isaac altars. He gives us the greatest blessing of all: His victorious presence bringing complete peace. "The more perfect is our self-surrender, the more perfect is our peace."[1]

We can join Paul in his declaration: we own nothing, and yet we have everything (see 2 Cor. 6:10). When we are in tune with the Lord's presence, we become partakers of all that Jesus is for us. We have peace that reigns victorious over our questions, disappointments, pain, fear, doubts, and discouragements. We release the last of our worries from within our grip, raising our hands in freedom and declaring, "This much, oh God, I love You!"

COMPLETE SURRENDER

Pain and desperate need bring God's truth to our awareness in a way that comfort and self-sufficiency do not. When life is hard, we may feel that God has abandoned us. But we believe that lie only because our line of communication with God is blocked by things we are afraid to surrender to Him.

Our home, at the top of a wooded mountain in a quiet suburb of Portland, Oregon, lacks strong cell-phone reception. As we drive farther and farther up the mountain toward our house through the trees and hills, more objects come between us and the cell tower, resulting in a weaker connection. But when we go down the mountain, closer to the towers, fewer objects are in the way, and we have a stronger connection. What a picture this is of our relationship with Jesus!

When we surrender to God the little idols that set up camp in the corners of our hearts, the volume of His voice goes up, the connection with Him is clear, and His message to us is sure: "I will never leave you or forsake you" (Heb. 13:5, HCSB). The lie that we have been abandoned is destroyed by His voice of truth within. We become aware of what is true for God's children: we are completely dependent on God for all things at all times. Abraham modeled what total dependence looked like when he strapped down his only son to be sacrificed on the altar.

Though his seventeenth-century language sometimes has me paging through my dictionary, I value the writings of Francois Fénelon, a French archbishop, theologian, and writer. His letters have taken me deeper into the sea of complete surrender:

> Often all that we offer to God is not that which He wills. What He desires most is what we are least willing to give Him, and that we dread to have Him ask of us. It is Isaac, the only son, the well-beloved, that He commands us to resign; all the rest is nothing in His sight, and He lets it be painful and fruitless, because His blessing is not upon the labor of a divided soul; it is His will that we should yield everything to Him; and short of this, there is no repose.[2] If you would prosper, and have God's blessing on your work, withhold nothing, cut to the quick, burn, spare nothing, and the God of peace will be with you. What consolation, what liberty, what strength, what enlargement of heart, what growth in grace, when there is nothing left between God and the soul, and when we have offered everything to Him to the uttermost, without hesitation.[3]

In our desire to live in unbroken fellowship with our Creator, surrender is vital. It is a daily, ongoing, moment-by-moment release of everything we are into our Father's hands. I wake up each day painfully aware of the cares of this world, temptations, and aches all around. Hunger for alone time with Jesus pulls me into my prayer closet, where I can release all that concerns me onto the

Isaac altar each morning. "Entire surrender to Jesus is the secret of perfect rest. Giving up one's whole life to Him, for Him alone to rule and order it, taking up His Yoke and submitting to be led and taught."[4]

Placing all we have upon the Isaac altar tunes us in to hear the voice of God so that we can consider what resides in the temples of our hearts, our worship center, and ask the Lord to cleanse them and fill every nook and cranny with Himself. By placing everything on the altar, we give Him all, and we realize, "Wow, our hands are *full*—full of *Him*, full of His love."

Suddenly we are taking on His work instead of our own or other people's, which means that His energy will be powerfully at work within us. He becomes our prioritizer, showing us how He desires for us to spend the time and energy that He grants us for kingdom glory. Giants that seemed insurmountable take on the shape of small weeds, easily plucked.

The courageous first step toward full surrender is dropping the desire to have everything figured out and instead choosing minute by minute to wait on God, who never disappoints. As we come to Him poor in spirit (see Matt. 5:3), understanding that nothing is ours and that we are entitled to nothing, we can release our nearest and dearest treasures to our Creator.

RECOGNIZING GOD'S POWER OVER ALL

While listening to the rhythm of my feet crunching leaves as I jogged, the Whisper came: *"Healing is about letting go."* This was followed by a vision of God's hand: through the eyes of my soul, I saw God's hand holding my life.

The Spirit brought to my mind Job 12:10: "In his hand is the life of every living thing and the breath of all mankind" (ESV). Isaiah 42:5 echoes this truth: "God, the LORD, created the heavens and stretched them out. He created the earth and everything in it. He gives breath to everyone, life to everyone who walks the earth." That quiet morning on the mountain trails, the Lord asked me to let go of my incessant planning and failed attempts to bring my own version of His beauty out of the hardships that have come into my life. How gently our Father was teaching me that He had never asked me to redeem my own trials. That was His territory!

The strongest Whispers come when I am living in full surrender, seeking first the kingdom of God. Concerning a revival that took place in South Africa in 1861, Andrew Murray wrote, "Oh, if we did not so often hinder Him with our much serving, and *much trying* to serve, how surely and mightily He would accomplish *His own work* of renewing souls into the likeness of Christ Jesus. What secrets He himself would whisper into the silence of a waiting heart."[5]

His desire for me is simply to love—to love Him and love others with His love. I am not to make it my aim to *do* great things for God but rather to seek Him with my whole heart and respond with trust and obedience to His Whisper within. I am to submit to His loving transformation of me into the image of His Son. Oh, to hold fast to the truth that there is only *one* Redeemer, *one* Creator, *one* upholder—and it is not me! This is true freedom in Christ. God's authority over all frees me to simply love and be loved.

LAYING DOWN OUR THINKING

Being both a deep thinker and a deep feeler leaves me in desperate need of daily communion with Jesus. I crumple without continual conversation with Him. He reminds me that I am fearfully and wonderfully made (see Ps. 139:14). He made me a sensitive soul for His purposes, and I can trust Him with it. I *will* trust Him with it.

Only by God's help can I obey the directive, "Stop thinking." I think all the time—*all* the time. I even think about how much

I'm thinking! Thanks be to God, we have a Savior who keeps us safe. He gives us His Word to hide in our hearts so we can be set free by channeling all our thinking into thoughts of the truth, love, goodness, and beauty of Jesus.

When my mind feels busy, I ask Jesus to take His gentle hands and hold my brain, absorbing the army of thoughts bouncing this way and that. Then I ask Him to put His tender hands right on my heart, hold anything that hurts, and heal the pain that no one sees.

We are commanded to trust in the Lord with *all* our hearts and not lean on our own understanding (see Prov. 3:5). With the help of the Spirit within us, we can trade our questions and hurts and frustrations for the truth that it's the giver, not the gift, who is our true treasure! While we wait for Him to move, we can rest in knowing that He is our inheritance and our portion (see Ps. 16:5). When the tribe of Levi was given their allotment, they received Jesus Himself. It was just as when the Lord told Abraham, "I am . . . your very great reward" (Gen. 15:1, NIV). As God's children, we can follow in the footsteps of the Levites, receiving Jesus as our portion (see Josh. 13:33).

When our minds are hammered by life's struggles and disappointments, we can hold fast to this truth: this world is not our home. Our promised inheritance is imperishable, undefiled, and unfading, kept in heaven for us (see 1 Pet. 1:4). It was Abraham's belief in God's character that placed his precious Isaac upon the altar that day and declared the Lord as his very great reward. Abraham trusted God to fulfill every promise made in whatever way He chose to do it.

When Waiting Gets Long

We are immersed in an Instacart culture that lets us shop online for products from local stores with guaranteed two-hour delivery.

We are losing opportunities within normal life to practice waiting. My children think that just about anything can be purchased on Amazon and will arrive on our front porch within a day, or even less if they choose same-day delivery!

Waiting is not easy, especially when life hurts or when our waiting concerns the people closest to us. Our vulnerable spots are the hardest to place on the Isaac altar. Perhaps we have bravely put something on the Isaac altar, but rather than receiving our answer right away, as Abraham did, we are still looking for that ram of deliverance! Worries become sticky during seasons of waiting, forming knots of anxiety as we get tied up in the "what if" outcomes concerning those we love.

The Isaac altar is a place of safe refuge for us when we are faced with fears, doubts, discouragement, and disappointments. We cry out hard tears, asking God to show us what we have taken off that altar and into our own hands.

I frequently retreat into nature, where I can watch the trees and clouds or listen to moving water, and I remind myself that God is always on the move, even when I cannot see or hear Him working. He is honored by our complete surrender, our tears of trust, and our waiting on the fulfillment of a word He spoke to us years ago. When the waiting gets long, kneeling below the Isaac altar with emptied hands helps me to trust Him. Returning often to His Word reminds me of His faithfulness, patience, and kindness. He is my trustworthy Father who is ever present for His girl. Our choice to trust becomes our voice of faith.

BEING EMPTIED TO BE FILLED

John 14 is a favorite spot for me to sit with Jesus and listen to Him speak. He promised us a gift: peace of mind and heart. But since it's a gift, that means we must put out our hands and receive it. That's the beauty of surrender—when we open our hands to let go of the things we cling to, we can then receive the fullness of the Spirit throughout our entire beings.

Being filled with Jesus' Spirit is receiving by faith what is already ours, not trying harder and harder to get it. It is also not "one and done" but rather an ongoing process that comes as a result of living in complete surrender to Him. Our emptying becomes our filling.

Being filled with the Spirit includes confessing and turning from our sin. The Spirit reigning in authority over us *will* change how we think and act. In *The Way to Pentecost*, Samuel Chadwick provides four steps that we can return to daily to be Spirit-filled believers: "All may be filled as full and as truly as the hundred and twenty on the day of Pentecost. The conditions are the same for all. Repent, Ask, Receive, Obey."[6] I have these four steps up on my prayer wall in the closet where I have my morning quiet times. I love Chadwick's gospel simplicity and emphasis on obedience: "The Spirit-filled must be Spirit-ruled."[7]

If we have given our hearts to Jesus, the *Spirit is in us*! But as I have drawn nearer to the Lord, I have begun to recognize the Holy Spirit as a *person* who is present, powerful, and willing and able to help me yield to Him: "God is a person and in the deep of His mighty nature He thinks, wills, enjoys, feels, loves, desires, and suffers as any other person may. In making Himself known to us, He stays by the familiar pattern of personality. He communicates with us through the avenues of our minds, our wills, and our emotions. The continuous and unembarrassed interchange of love and thought between God and the soul of the redeemed man is the throbbing heart of the New Testament religion."[8]

I recently enjoyed the biography of Andrew Murray, a nineteenth-century revivalist, missionary, and pastor. Murray's writings are excellent resources for digging deep into Spirit-filled living. He writes, "Being filled with the Spirit is simply this: having my whole nature yielded to His power. When the whole soul is yielded to the Holy Spirit, God Himself will fill it."[9] As we enter our quiet spaces to sit under the gentle searchlight of our Creator, He reveals things or people that we have not laid down in complete surrender. When we have not given up all, we cannot receive all that Jesus has to give.

God longs to fill us with His Spirit! Often people express to me that they don't feel the Holy Spirit intensely the way others seem to. That is okay! Faith is not a feeling. Surrender to Jesus opens the way for His Spirit to fill us, whether we feel ecstatic in the moment or not. I have often seen the quiet filling of the Spirit show up in me as complete confidence in God's authority over all my circumstances rather than as a jumping-up-and-down Holy Spirit moment. I do *love* the jumping-up-and-down moments! But if that was the only indicator of a life filled with the Spirit, we'd be in trouble!

We were given the incredible gift of the indwelling Holy Spirit, the source of holiness and happiness. As we surrender all to Him and partake of His Spirit, we will taste and see that the Lord is good (see Ps. 34:8). In reading John 14, we can see the oneness of our triune God, that perfect fellowship that He has within the Godhead that He has invited us into through the blood of His Son. As we give Him everything, He pulls in close and reminds us of what is true. We receive the strength that comes from His favor over us, which is grace that sustains and encourages our hearts.

God *will* reveal Himself to the yielded heart (see John 14:21, 23). We have the Spirit as our advocate and the One who leads us into all truth.

BRINGING OUR BOATS

Sam Storms's *Practicing the Power* teaches a beautiful way of viewing the work of the Holy Spirit as the wind that blows our boats. Our responsibility and daily sacrifice are to "bring our boats" to the lake each day, set them in the water, and pray. God is the One who controls the wind that will make our boats move.

Our family recently went on a trip to the San Juan Islands. We were staying on Lopez Island, near a lake. We noticed some canoes and paddleboats abandoned on the shore. When we asked about them at the visitors' center in town, we were delighted to hear that they were free for us to use!

My oldest son, Luke, wanted to row to the dock on the other side of the lake. Joining in with him in his excitement for the adventure at hand, I grabbed an oar and said, "Let's go!"

We put our whole selves into rowing, but somehow we didn't seem to be making much progress toward the dock. It had looked close enough, but I hadn't considered that the wind would be working against us. Sometimes when God isn't moving the way we hope, we will be tempted to pick up the oars to help Him out rather than trust and wait on the One whom even the wind and waves obey (see Matt. 8:27).

When waiting gets long, when hardship brings unanswered questions, we have the choice to bring our boats to the lake every day, praying persistently, like the tenacious widow in Luke 18:

One day Jesus told his disciples a story to show that they should always pray and never give up. "There was a judge in a certain city," he said, "who neither feared God nor cared about people. A widow of that city came to him repeatedly, saying, 'Give me justice in this dispute with my enemy.' The judge ignored her for a while, but finally he said to himself, 'I don't fear God or care about people, but this woman is driving me crazy. I'm going to see that she gets justice, because she is wearing me out with her constant requests!' "

Then the Lord said, "Learn a lesson from this unjust judge. Even he rendered a just decision in the end. So don't you think God will surely give justice to his chosen people who cry out to him day and night? Will he keep putting them off? I tell you, he will grant justice to them quickly!

But when the Son of Man returns, how many will he find on the earth who have faith?" (Luke 18:1–8)

Bringing our boats might mean getting up early, attending an event the Lord asks us to go to, or just showing up for a friend in need. Bringing our boats is putting into practice the gifts of the Spirit we have been given. We pray for healing, and we pray for deliverance. God will be in charge of the wind! We offer up our trust and our obedience, casting all outcomes on Him.

May the nearness of our Beloved be real to us within our storms. He is Creator and Savior. He is speaking, sustaining, and *coming* again. May we be found faithful, determined to trust Him. May we bring our questions and our pain to the One who alone is provider and defender. May we carry to the Savior those around us who are struggling the way friends carried to Jesus a paralyzed man on a mat (see Luke 5:17–26). The battle is the Lord's, but we have one powerful choice that is ours to make: will we raise our eyes, wearied by disappointments, in childlike trust to our perfect parent who longs to be gracious to us, to the One who will never disappoint?

When the hard stays hard and the rainbows vanish, our decisions to leave our Isaacs on that altar and trust God with everything raise broken hallelujahs to the Lord. As this pleasing aroma of sacrifice and sweet song rises, our Savior responds with a fresh wave of His love flooding our souls through His Whisper within—love that wins. He hears us. He sees us. He loves us. Always.

⟶ *Pray It In* ⟵

"Hear my prayer, O LORD; listen to my plea! Answer me because you are faithful and righteous. . . . I remember the days of old. I ponder all your great works and think about what you have done. I lift my hands to you in prayer. I thirst for you as parched land thirsts for rain" (Ps. 143:1, 5–6). Father, I cry to You as Jesus cried to You, "Father, all things are possible for you. Remove this cup from me. Yet not what I will, but what you will" (Mark 14:36, ESV). Jesus, thank You for taking hold of me today. I rest in Your love.

4

FASTING IN PURSUIT

Fasting is personal. It is a tender topic in our Christian culture. So why am I writing a chapter on fasting? Because fasting has rescued my soul from being stuck in darkness.

Fasting is a way to tangibly express our acceptance of Jesus' invitation to His table: "Come to me, all of you who are weary and carry heavy burdens, and I will give you rest. Take my yoke upon you. Let me teach you, because I am humble and gentle at heart, and you will find rest for your souls" (Matt. 11:28–29).

Through periodic fasting I have experienced a deeper filling of the Spirit than I have ever known before. God's voice has grown clearer, resulting in perspective changes, comfort, help for decisions regarding healthcare, and guidance in relationships. I have been lifted from pits of despair. Darkened corners of my heart have been illuminated and swept clean.

Fasting sparks in us a deeper desire for God Himself. When we fast in order to seek God, when He is our deepest longing, His answer to us is *yes* for more of Himself. As His Spirit fills us to overflowing, we become vessels of His love.

Fasting for spiritual purposes is not about deprivation as much as it is about pursuit. This is not a chapter on medical fasting, although because we are three-part beings (body, soul, and spirit), our bodies *will* be affected when we fast for spiritual purposes. However, there is a stark contrast between the motives for spiritual fasting and the reasons for medical fasting. This chapter will speak specifically to fasting for spiritual purposes.[1]

Through fasting we can experience the goodness of God and true freedom that comes as a result of chains breaking. Things that have had a hold on us as long as we can remember will lose their lure. In each of our unique journeys, fasting will take us deeper with God and help us taste His goodness over whatever it is that occupies our thoughts, fills our insides, and takes up our time.

Fasting is between us and God. The Spirit reveals to us, when we earnestly ask Him, what we are placing above God in our hearts and thus need to fast from (see 1 John 5:21). Fasting is not limited to food. In our culture today we reach for countless things to stuff those painful places in our souls that God longs to fill with Himself. Filling ourselves with these things makes less room for the Spirit; fasting from these things can lead to a deeper communion with the Spirit.

My first taste of fasting came as a result of a desperate desire to hear God's voice. I experienced God's goodness in a new and delightful way while fasting from one meal per day. This time of fasting was not a depriving but a feasting. It was not a suppression of appetite but the development of an increasingly insatiable appetite. It was not a no but a yes, a pursuit of God Himself through feasting on His Word and prolonged, private communing with Him.

My desire is to know God deeper, to enjoy Him, to be intensely aware of His constant holding of me and His love song over me. With each small fast I recognize the truth that Jesus fulfills me far more than hanging out with my phone, those extra minutes of sleep, a few more Google searches, a cup of tea or coffee, squeezing in more hours of work, a bite of dark chocolate, a long run, or perhaps even breakfast or lunch or dinner. There is nothing wrong with fully delighting in these gifts from the Lord! But oh, how quickly we can stray from enjoying the gifts *with* God to partaking of them without any thought of His presence and power within us.

FASTING INCREASES OUR DESIRES FOR GOD

We have two small indoor house plants that have somehow survived my forgetful care over the last three years. The other day both plants were begging for water, with every leaf lying limp. With just a little water and light from some time sitting by the window, they perked right up!

When we lived in Southern California, the heat easily reached triple digits week after week in the summer. Gideon, our golden retriever puppy, was not a huge fan of the extreme heat. His breathing would intensify rapidly as the heat dehydrated him. Panting louder and louder, he would look everywhere for drops of water as we neared the doggy water fountain by the park trail. Remembering how Gideon longed for water in the summer heat reminds me of how desperate I am for God in the heat of trial. I thirst for the living God, the One who completely understands the difficulties I face. "As the deer longs for streams of water, so I long for you, O God. I thirst for God, the living God. When can I go and stand before him?" (Ps. 42:1–2).

Our fasting is our earnest asking for more of Jesus, for Him to return, and for His presence to be powerfully experienced in the midst of our moments. It protects us from desires for other things that enter in and choke out the Word (see Mark 4:19), because fasting intensifies our desire for God Himself!

FASTING SENSITIZES OUR EARS TO GOD'S VOICE

Fasting has been a means of sensitizing my ear to God's voice, giving me wisdom for decisions that I have needed to make in all areas of my life. Fasting has deepened my longing for God. My dehydrated soul finds all it needs in Jesus when I am in a position of fasting. My mind, will, and emotions are satisfied when I earnestly seek God—not His gifts but Himself (see Ps. 63:1–5).

John Piper's *A Hunger for God* transformed my thinking about fasting. I have been through it four times now and still find new truths in it that set me free and move me closer to God through deepening love. Pastor John teaches that fasting is actually feasting. It's about fervent asking—an intense longing for more and more of Jesus: "What we hunger for most, we worship."[2] Denying ourselves, for a season, of our smartphones and devices, food or drink, being overly committed, an extra hour of sleep can increase our hunger for God Himself. "When God is the supreme hunger of our hearts, He will be supreme in everything."[3]

"The strongest, most mature Christians I have ever met are the hungriest for God. It might seem that those who eat most would be least hungry. But that's not the way it works with an inexhaustible fountain, an infinite feast, and a glorious God."[4]

FASTING BRINGS FREEDOM

Fasting brings freedom! The cords of sin that bind us are broken when we condition our appetites to be hungry for *God* Himself, not God's gifts. Galatians 5:13 cautions us to use the freedom that we have in Christ not to satisfy the desires of our sin nature but to serve one another in love. Is the activity or substance we are about to partake of joyful worship or chained misery? This will shine a light into the areas in our souls where we think we have freedom but in reality are chained by a habit. We are slaves to whatever has mastery over us. Fasting fosters holy habits. Through it our life choices begin reflecting the one life we are called to emulate—that of Jesus Christ.

Fasting is earnest asking that reflects our total dependence on God. It's not about a fight to say no; it's about choosing His yes.

The most important choice we make each morning is the decision to "click in." When my husband, Steve, heads out on his road bike, his ride is most enjoyable when he first takes the time to put on his special shoes made for cycling. They are designed to click into the pedals, strengthening his power source and the effectiveness of pedaling. It's much like when we make the subtle yet powerful and life-altering choice to click into the Spirit each day. Rather than trying harder, Christ's divine power flows through us as we live under the authority of our new master, God the Holy Spirit.

New layers of areas that need to change in us are exposed bit by bit as the Spirit reveals them to us through fasting. These areas are dominated by something other than Jesus. First Corinthians 6:12 teaches us that although all things are lawful for us, they aren't all helpful! Paul commits to not being dominated by anything.

What dominates our minds? Our hearts? When we choose God over these things, our hunger and longing for Him grow. Our awareness of His Spirit's power and presence within us explodes! I have been surprised by the freedom that the Holy Spirit has brought me in response to my intense asking.

Enslaved no longer because of the blood of Jesus, we have the freedom to partake of the Lord's gifts and abstain from whatever we need to lay down. When the Lord sets us free, we will be free indeed (see John 8:36)!

FASTING CREATES A DOMINO EFFECT

Choosing to discipline ourselves in one area of life, such as placing limits on smartphone usage, tends to create a domino effect in other areas of our lives. We feel lighter due to the increased freedom that comes from living untethered to our devices. Our energy increases as our emotional loads dwindle when our intake of digital communication is paused or significantly reduced. We begin to wonder what life would be like if we had this same freedom in how we eat, how we sleep, and what activities and relationships we commit to.

Because we are body, spirit, and soul, the spiritual disciplines absolutely affect our bodies, and the physical disciplines hugely impact our souls. Sleep, nutrition, exercise, stress relief, laughing with a friend, receiving hugs, not stuffing our emotions—*all* impact both ways: body to soul and soul to body.

Holding back one habit in our lives from the transforming love the Holy Spirit longs to breathe into our whole beings will cast a shadow on our entire souls. Matthew Parker's song "Shadowlands" speaks of the shadow that such sin creates. This walled-off corner starts to fester; then it infects our souls like a paralyzing virus, reducing our capacity to hear the Whisper within. We become the choices that we make, sometimes slowly, sometimes quickly. The little decisions we make throughout our moments add up over time to create big changes or big problems. Whether we decide not to buy things on credit or to get up five minutes earlier than usual to pray, over the course of one year we will see big results. Little decisions matter.

Our choice to obey is an outward manifestation of an inward position. We have received forgiveness and been set free. "Shadowlands" has been a favorite song of mine, especially at Christmastime, when we celebrate freedom from the land of shadows! Jesus came to be light in our entire beings. Our sin doesn't stop His love, but it creates a shadow that darkens our sense of God's presence, making us feel separated from God. Jesus came as light, to forgive and free us from the shadows.

Our position is that we are His beloved. We can take a deep breath and speak this truth: "I am loved." This truth creates a domino effect of lives that love God and love others. "We love because He first loved us" (1 John 4:19, ESV). This love produces an intense desire to obey Him with our whole hearts (see John 14:15). This obedience guides our intense asking when we are in a place of fasting.

I often find my prayer requests changing to fervent praise and adoration when I am fasting. Sometimes the Spirit takes over, causing a 180-degree turn in what I am asking for. First John 3:22 is an excellent passage to meditate on during our intense asking: "We will receive from him whatever we ask because we obey him and do the things that please him." The domino effect triggered by wholehearted obedience is asking in the name of Jesus for what brings glory to the Father. Fasting produces asking that glorifies the Father (see John 14:13).

Fasting Brings Encouragement

Sometimes we are so low that we can't begin to imagine fasting at all. Change feels far away. We falter when we sin—*again*. But no discipline in the Christian life is one and done but rather a lifestyle of asking, seeking, and knocking. God meets us where we are. As our loving Father, He desires to hear from us, always!

If my children grew discouraged that they had messed up *again* and stopped coming to me for forgiveness, I'd be devastated! How much more so our perfect Father, who is ready with arms wide open to bear hug us right back to Himself, our safe place. It is the Father's gentleness that makes us great (see Ps. 18:35). How comforting to know that His ways are tender, kind, and infinitely patient. "Great is our Lord, and abundant in power; his understanding is beyond measure" (Ps. 147:5, ESV). There is no pit of discouragement too deep for God's presence to enter.

Jeremiah, the weeping prophet, gave us an action step to take when discouragement hits: "This I call to mind, and therefore

I have hope: The steadfast love of the LORD never ceases; his mercies never come to an end; they are new every morning; great is your faithfulness. 'The LORD is my portion,' says my soul, 'therefore I will hope in him.' The LORD is good to those who wait for him, to the soul who seeks him" (Lam. 3:21–24, ESV). This is an action step: calling to mind, remembering—beginning to praise God for all He has done and who He is.

David took similar steps in expressing his pain and then choosing to remember who God is: "I am deeply discouraged, but I will remember you" (Ps. 42:6)! He still saw waves coming over his head in verse 7. But he declared that even then, the Lord was pouring out His unfailing love on him, and through the night the Lord kept David company as David prayed to the God who gave him life (see Ps. 42:8).

In the cloudy skies of discouragement, fasting has helped me see with more clarity what God *has* done for me. It seems fasting from my devices, like my smartphone and computer, is especially helpful in restoring my closeness with Jesus. Without the practice of fasting, during times of heavy discouragement, the Whisper within me grows too quiet. I find it difficult to make out His voice amidst my spiraling thoughts heading downward into despair. Sometimes it helps me to clear my schedule of all that can be canceled or postponed for a couple days to create quiet spaces and retreat as often as possible into the Word of God with the Spirit as my comforter.

In times of despair, we too quickly turn to our phones, where we are filled with everyone else's thoughts and advice, causing us to lose the voice that matters most within the mayhem.

FASTING BRINGS PEACE

Our Father keeps us in His Son, Jesus, who Himself is our peace (see Eph. 2:14). "Blessed is the man who trusts in the LORD, and whose hope *is* the LORD. For he will be like a tree planted by the water, which spreads out its roots by the river, and will not fear when heat comes; but its leaf will be green, and will not be anxious in the year of drought, nor will cease from yielding fruit" (Jer. 17:7–8, NKJV). "The godly have deep roots" (Prov. 12:3).

Fasting while receiving the Scripture as soul food grows a deep root system to hold us firm and keep us encouraged through the strong winds of affliction.

Often during times of fasting, we are given eyes to see areas in our hearts that are not fully surrendered to our Beloved. With loving-kindness, He moves us toward repentance. He gently begins to wipe clean those dusty places, filling them up with Himself. Holiness in us increases as we become more like Him.

Numerous times when I have been troubled in my soul, taking a day away from my phone, computer, commitments, food, or whatever it takes and turning my focus to Jesus and His Word have reset me. Jesus resumes His reign as King of my whole heart and brings His peace along with Him, for He promises great peace for those who love His Word (see Ps. 119:165).

THE ISAIAH 58 FAST

In March 2019, my husband, Steve, and I were led into what we called our Isaiah 58 fast. This was in the weeks leading up to Easter Sunday, when we would then celebrate the joy of resurrection power. This resurrection power is promised in God's Word to break every chain!

Each morning during those weeks, I read the same passage, Isaiah 58:6–13, in as many translations as I could find. Then I sat and asked the Spirit to teach me what the passage meant and how my life should change in response to it. I wrote out each command in this passage along with every promise. This was the *Word* of God, and out of my love for God, which is from His love for me, I wanted to obey every action to which He was calling me.

The fast that God chooses (the Isaiah 58 fast) is to:

- Loose the bonds of wickedness
- Undo heavy burdens
- Let the oppressed go free
- Break every yoke
- Share our bread with the hungry
- Bring the poor and those who are cast out into our homes
- Clothe the naked
- Not hide ourselves from our own flesh (turn away from our own flesh and blood)
- Take away the yoke from our midst
- Stop pointing fingers
- Extend ours souls to the hungry
- Satisfy the afflicted soul
- Turn away from doing our own pleasure on the Sabbath day; call the Sabbath a delight; honor God rather than going our own ways, not finding our own pleasure or speaking our own words

Steve and I came before the Lord to ask Him to point out the "yokes" that needed to be broken in our lives during this time. Sin is like a sneaky tentacle, quietly and slowly wrapping itself around us, choking off the free-flowing connection to the Spirit within our entire beings.

Only the Spirit could tenderly show us where we had begun to point fingers or turn away from our own flesh and blood. We were reminded of the importance of seeking God on the Sabbath. It was not law but love leading us to turn off our phones each weekend, giving ourselves a quiet space for a deeper connection with God.

The fast that God chooses, mentioned in Isaiah 58, is followed by the truth that God's arm is never too short to save nor His ear too dull to hear, but our sin places distance between us and God (see Isa. 59:1–2). We become less aware of His presence and His resurrection power when sin is distancing us from His heart. Satan would love to destroy us, especially those who are living and speaking His message, and as Steve likes to say, Satan plays dirty. We have worldly influences to war against as well. Not only that, but we have another enemy: our own selves. Boy, Mrs. Self can be a real annoyance to me! Our power against all these enemies is to pray in the Spirit *with* the sword of the Spirit.

That is the victorious life in Jesus Christ! A life free from the habitual sin that chokes off the blessings from our Father.

When Steve and I committed to the Isaiah 58 fast, the promises to us were these:

- Our light would break forth like the morning, like dawn in the darkness.
- Our healing would spring forth speedily.
- God's righteousness would go before us.
- The glory of the Lord would be our rear guard.
- We would call, and the Lord would answer.
  We would cry, and He would say, "Here I am!"
- The Lord would guide us continually.
- The Lord would satisfy our souls in drought.
- The Lord would strengthen our bones.
- We would be like a well-watered garden.
- We would be like springs of water whose waters do not fail.
- We would be known as a rebuilder of walls and a restorer of homes.
- We would delight ourselves in the Lord. He would cause us to ride on the high hills of the earth.

"The mouth of the LORD has spoken" (Isa. 58:14, ESV).

THE EZRA FAST:
SEEKING GOD'S PROTECTION, BLESSING, AND DIRECTION

Another excellent example of biblical fasting and the blessings to be received through it are found in Ezra 8. This passage taught me the power of the pause—to stop and earnestly ask God for direction when arriving at life's intersections. I learned to proceed with caution only after diligently asking God to show us the path He desired us to take and to take time to seek His provision and protection for the road ahead.

The example comes from Ezra, who declared a fast in order to seek God's presence and to ask for God's protection and provision as he led the second group of exiles home to Jerusalem:

> I proclaimed a fast there at the river of Ahava, that we might humble ourselves before our God, to seek from Him the right way for us and our little ones and all our possessions. For I was ashamed to request of the king an escort of soldiers and horsemen to help us against the enemy on the road, because we had spoken to the king, saying, "The hand of our God is upon all those for good who seek Him, but His power and His wrath are against all those who forsake Him." So we fasted and entreated our God for this, and He answered our prayer. (Ezra 8:21–24, NKJV)

Traveling down a few verses, we see what God did for Ezra in response to his earnest asking: "We departed from the river of Ahava on the twelfth day of the first month, to go to Jerusalem. And the hand of our God was upon us, and He delivered us from the hand of the enemy and from ambush along the road" (Ezra 8:31, NKJV). Fasting is a tangible way of declaring our earnest desire for God's presence and power over our lives.

HELP! ALL ODDS ARE AGAINST US!

One last example of biblical fasting, found in the book of Esther, provides an excellent example of fasting when we are faced with an "all odds are against me" situation. A decree had been sent out that all the Jewish people were to be killed (see Esth. 3:13). When this news reached Queen Esther, she declared a three-day fast to prepare for going before the king, uninvited, to request his help. This was dangerous! She was only to see the king at *his* invitation! So Esther prepared by fasting, fervently asking God to move on behalf of her people (see Esth. 4:16). God responded by not only protecting Esther but also by using her courage to save the Jewish people (see Esth. 5:2; 8:5–17).

Fasting puts us in a place of exceptional closeness with God as we desire Him, His will, and His ways above all else. When I have faced major life decisions, I have never had the Lord *not* provide wisdom when I have surrendered all and been in a position of humble and fervent asking. I have spent days reading the same passages over and over, praying them, and meditating on them. Some of my go-to favorites are Proverbs 3:1–18, Proverbs 4:20–27, Daniel 2:18–23, and Psalm 23.

Fasting produces believing prayers as we take in the Word of God as our living bread and are changed by the Word as we pray. "Sanctify them in the truth; your word is truth" (John 17:17, ESV). Such believing prayers are never forced by trying hard to believe for something we want. They are a natural byproduct of faith that comes by hearing, which comes by the Word of God (see Rom. 10:17). We hunger for His will and His ways above our phones, food, busyness, and anything or anyone that distracts us from private communion with Him.

In the four steps to a Spirit-filled life that I mentioned in chapter 3—repent, ask, receive, obey—biblical fasting is a way to express the intensity with which we are repenting and asking. God does not need us to do something huge; He is honored by our declaration with some simple fast. "This much, O God, I want you!"[5] Fasting in pursuit of God results in being filled with His Spirit and resting in our Creator's love.

Pray It In

My ways are before Your eyes, Adonai; You observe all my paths. Release me from cords of sin that would hold me down (see Prov. 5:21–22). I meditate on You day and night and receive strength of soul; I know that You will keep me from requests that are not from You and would send leanness into my soul (see Ps. 106:15)! You satisfy the longing soul and fill the hungry with good things (see Ps. 107:9). Oh Father, make me hungry for You, for You fill me (see Matt. 5:6). Bend down, oh Lord, and hear my prayer; answer me, for I need Your help. Father, fill me with joy and goodness in You as I search for You (see Ps. 40:16–17).

Jesus, thank You for taking hold of me today. I rest in Your love.

5

VOICE RECOGNITION

We face uncertainty when we arrive at life's crossroads. Who do we listen to? Which way should we go?

Our souls are battlegrounds. The voices in them can be loud, or they can be quiet and subtle. And they can be antagonistic. The enemy's voice mingles with good old self, our sin nature and inner critic. Throw in text messages, e-mails, the Internet, and other forms of written communication, and our souls can be anything but the flowing peaceful rivers we crave.

Speaking the gentle yet fierce name of Jesus out loud is an effective weapon against chaos in our souls. Just saying His name aloud evacuates our souls of every evil presence around us. When we submit to God, the enemy flees (see James 4:7). Speaking His name out loud, "Jesus," reminds us that He is near us, willing and able to help. As we say His name, He settles the thoughts causing unrest in our souls and draws our thoughts to His voice.

How do we respond when a friend calls us up to say, as one of mine did a few years ago, "Lisa, I just heard about a healer coming to a city a couple hours away. You have to be there in person to receive your healing, so make sure you're there at eleven tonight!"

In that moment, my mind swirled. "Is this amazing miracle cure being offered at this church tonight the real deal? If I can't make it there, does that mean I miss out? And why do I need to be there so late?" I hung up the phone that evening in turmoil. I trusted this friend. I also believe in miraculous healing. Yet I was exhausted and simply wanted to go to bed. My entire being *wanted* to believe that if I just got in the car and drove down to this place, my cancer troubles would be over, but I couldn't turn off the disturbing light blinking red in my troubled soul: "*Warning, warning.*"

"Jesus? Jesus. Show me the way, Lord!"

DISCERNING TRUTH FROM LIES

While I believe with all my heart in miracles and in asking for them, I did not get in the car that night to drive two hours to the healing service. When I spoke the name of Jesus out loud, pleading with Him to show me if I should go, the Spirit nudged me to stay home.

Since that night several years ago, the Lord has helped me remember the importance of taking time to ask Him for His guidance. The flesh wants to rush, especially when it is afflicted, but the Spirit is not in a hurry. Yes, the Spirit might ask me to drive two hours to be prayed over for healing, but being told that I needed to go instantly, in the middle of the night? That thought troubled my soul and encouraged me to take time to ask Jesus to help me discern truth from lies.

One way to recognize what is true is to make sure that what we are hearing is in full agreement with the written Word of God. God's Word is truth (see John 17:17). The Whisper within, the gentle voice of the Holy Spirit, will always align with truth. Nothing we hear from the Spirit of God will ever disagree with the written Word of God. Ever. We are not to believe every spirit, but we are to test the spirits to see whether they are from God (see 1 John 4:1). We are commanded to test *everything*, hold onto what is good, and abstain from all that is evil (see 1 Thess. 5:21–22).

This is why time in God's Word is vital. How can we know whether something is true if we do not know what truth is? The Holy Spirit is given to guide us into all truth. We must test every voice by the written Word of God—including every single word in *this* book. We should never listen to something said by anyone, even someone we trust, without making sure that his or her words line up with Scripture.

I have heard people say that we can simply claim healing and God will heal us. And I have seen God heal people in answer to believing prayer! But I have also known others who believed with all their hearts for healing yet did not receive the answer they desired. My own cancer journey, combined with the experiences of others dear to my heart who are facing cancer, has led me to wrestle with the question "What *do* I believe about divine healing?" That question sent me on a search through Scripture on my knees before the Lord, pleading to be taught truth—yes, about healing but also about how I should live the days I *have* been given.

We do not serve a God who ultimately serves us. I tremble writing that. He is a holy God, righteous and just in all He does. He is able to perform miracles, and He does not ever need to explain His ways to us. I tremble at His nearness, His bigness, His power, His love. From eternity to eternity, He *is God* (see Isa. 43:13).

Since 2015, I have hungered to study the gifts of the Spirit, asking God to help me recognize and exercise the grace gifts He has bestowed upon me. Nothing is ours. We are His. The gifts are His. Nothing is for our personal gain, but rather through death to self we are called to live through Jesus Christ.

God as a perfect parent takes a unique way with each of His children. He knows us better than we could ever know ourselves. He knows the right ways to teach us, discipline us, and use us for His greater kingdom work. He has a way of orchestrating circumstances that leave us in awe of His handiwork through divine appointments sprinkled throughout circumstances we would never have chosen for ourselves. Oh, the goodness of God in hardship astounds me!

My belief and personal experience are this: I will absolutely claim whatever the Spirit in me asks me to claim, for me or for others, that is in alignment with the Bible. What joy! When I read Sam Storms's book *Practicing the Power*, I began to pray, out of obedience, for every person I came across who was in need of healing, deliverance, and encouragement and was willing to receive prayer. As Christians, we follow in the footsteps of our teacher, Jesus Christ. In James 5:14–15, we are instructed to lay hands on the sick and pray for healing in Jesus' name. So we pray. We pray in complete faith in God's capacity to do whatever He wants, however He wants, whenever He wants, with or without our understanding.

I have had experiences of "God bumps" (my name for explosive goose bumps all over my body when God moves) when praying for healing and a person was healed. That was *not* me. All healing comes from Jesus, who alone receives all the glory; we are simply His vessels. I have also had people I prayed over die from cancer and receive their completion of healing at eternity's shore. There is much that I do not understand. But one thing I do know: obedience is always the best way. After that comes trust.

I believe in miracles. I always will. Miraculous is the character of my God, the author of miracles, who is the same yesterday, today, and forever. There is no disease that Jesus is not able to completely cure. I pray regularly for long life to be Steve's helpmate and to raise up my four arrows, Luke, Ellie, Gracie, and Sammy J, to love and follow Jesus all their days. I pray that what I pray for will be the desires of God within me. I believe that God *does* give us the desires of our hearts when we are completely delighting in Him as the King of our hearts, living as love slaves to our Beloved (see Ps. 37:4). *El Elyon*, God Most High, is not to be reduced to a genie in a bottle to grant our every wish.

Oh, how I long to be steadfast in sitting in hushed stillness before the Lord, aware of His presence. When I do, I begin praying the Word in the Spirit and follow the Spirit's leading. Our prayers are heard by a holy God who will respond to us, but our prayers will *never change God*. God will be God, the same yesterday, today, and forever. But prayer will change *us*. Never have I had peace when my soul is in chaos with too many voices speaking at once. Only the gentle voice of Jesus within us can grant calm in our souls even when the hurricane winds in life are blowing.

FOUR TESTS FOR DISCERNING FALSE TEACHING

My tears mixed with the rain falling from the stormy Northwest skies as I climbed into my car to leave my first, and last, appointment with a holistic doctor. Voices crowded my head. Shock shook my hands. Another door for medical help closed. *Yet* there it was—rejoicing rising up from within my soul! I rejoiced because my Father had protected me. The Whisper within had become a shout echoing off the walls of that home-based medical office. I had just experienced the truth of Jesus' promise that we are not to worry in advance about what we will say when we are brought under persecution, for He will give us the words (see Matt. 10:19).

Steve and I had been excited about the thought of an outside-the-box physician to help me with some of the health problems I have struggled with for years. Yet I felt caution as I drove to the appointment to meet this new doctor. I had reached out to a couple close friends and mentors, asking them to pray this one specific request: that Jesus would let me know if this person and place were spiritually safe for me.

God answered this prayer loud and clear. After taking my seat in the waiting room, I noticed a box lying next to my chair labeled "Angel Cards." That was the first trigger that caused my eyebrows to rise in question. Then came another after another as I took in my surroundings and overheard conversations from the back room: the physician and the patient were talking to angels, addressing them by name. While I could not mentally process everything I was seeing and hearing, I sensed the Spirit telling me, "*Get out!*" I sat with shaky hands, my patient paperwork half filled out, praying, "Jesus, *help!*"

What happened next can only be described as God taking full possession of me. Peace propelled my feet to the physician's little office in the back. Before my appointment even started, it ended. Standing in the office doorway, I thanked the physician for her time. I stated that I was spiritually unsafe there and would be leaving.

She turned her piercing gaze on me, responding intensely, "Excuse me, but *I am* a Christian. *My* husband is a priest at the largest church in this area! I am not only a Christian but also a prophet, anointed to heal. I believe that Christ is in all humans, whether Muslim or atheist or nothing." She claimed that she called out the Christ in everyone, and that was how she healed people. "We are all the same," she said, "so how could I be unsafe?" She stared into my eyes. "You are obviously not ready for the healing I could give you."

The Holy Spirit calmed me instantly, guiding my response: "Jesus is my healer. He can bring complete healing to me however and whenever He wants."

She argued, "No, it doesn't work that way. Jesus doesn't just wave a wand and make it happen. *I* make the healing happen." Hmm. No, I have seen case after case in the written Word of God where, yes, Jesus did just simply heal! Yes, He uses doctors but, no, He doesn't have to explain Himself if He chooses not to!

I let the woman know that in order to be a Christian, a Christ follower, we must repent of our sins and ask Jesus to forgive us and be Lord of our lives. I told her that because I had given my heart to Jesus, I had His very Spirit within me, guiding me, and He was letting me know that I needed to leave now. I thanked her for her kindness in scheduling me. Then I walked out, got into my car, and drove away.

That conversation branded upon my heart the truth that some of the most dangerous voices we will encounter contain thick lies wrapped in a thin layer of palatable truth. Satan himself masquerades as an angel of light (see 2 Cor. 11:14).

In His goodness, just three days prior to my appointment with the holistic doctor, Jesus had put into my hands Pastor Jerry Rueb's *Defending the Flock of God: Unmasking the Threat of False Teaching.* For more than forty-five years Pastor Jerry has been a truth-teaching shepherd, under Jesus, that great shepherd of the sheep, to thousands through his local church and global ministries. I devoured his book in three days, not knowing that God was using what I was reading to sharpen my awareness of false teaching. Pastor Jerry shared four tests that we should put all teaching and teachers through to unmask even the most well-disguised lies. The same discernment that the Word of God and His Spirit give us to unmask false teachers is the discernment God grants us to recognize *truth* teachers—those whose teaching aligns with God's Word and whose character reflects the character of Jesus.

Here is a brief summary of the four tests "that enable us to accurately discern false teachers and expose their false doctrines":[1]

1. *The doctrinal test.* Ask the question "Is what we are seeing or hearing doctrinally consistent with Scripture?" The Word of God is the standard by which all teaching must be measured; it is the court of last appeal and the final authority in all matters of faith or practice. For a standard to be effective and trustworthy, it must have four qualities: it must be

perfect, reliable, complete, and forever unchanging. The Bible is the only standard that measures up to all four of these qualities.

2. *The personal test.* Evaluate a teacher's personal life: "Is the person making this claim credible and also accountable to God?" Investigate the character, behavior, motivation, and lifestyle of every teacher, "apostle," or "prophet." Christlike character, not talk, is the essence of the personal test. Look for humility—for God glorification versus self-promotion.

3. *The spiritual test.* What evidence is there that the source of this message is the Holy Spirit? Behind every teaching there is a spirit; we must test each one to see if it is from God! "Dear friends, do not believe everyone who claims to speak by the Spirit. You must test them to see if the spirit they have comes from God. For there are many false prophets in the world" (1 John 4:1).

4. *The evidential test.* Is there evidence that the teaching and the teacher's life are bearing fruit that glorifies God? Jesus teaches us that we will recognize false teachers by their fruit (see Matt. 7:20).[2]

We need to look for the Spirit's fruit in the lives of our spiritual mentors, music leaders, preaching pastors, and Bible-study leaders. Do we sense a person of humility, who is completely dependent on God for all things? The most humble people I know are the ones who leave me hungering deeply for more of God. I see fruit in their lives that I long for in my own life. They consistently point people to God through their words and lifestyle. "But those who exalt themselves will be humbled, and those who humble themselves will be exalted" (Matt. 23:12).

When worship leaders exhibit the fruit of humility, they become vessels pointing us to Christ rather than distractions onstage. When fruit-filled teachers speak, they speak as though they are speaking the very words of God (see 1 Pet. 4:11). As Pastor Jerry has often taught (I listen to him online often!), the most dangerous voices are the ones that appear to be 95 percent right. We must plead with the Lord for discernment in all things at all times. He will give it! We must also hide His Word in our hearts. The Spirit will bring these words of God to mind in our moments of need when we cry out, "Jesus, *help!*" Jesus set the example in Matthew 4 when He used the sword of the Spirit as His defense (see Matt. 4:1–11).

After the spiritual high I initially felt upon leaving the doctor's office—something that often happens after the Holy Spirit takes over and does a work through us—doubts began to echo in the now quieted battlefield of my soul: *Is there any physician who can help resolve my chronic health struggles? Am I doing all the right things in healthcare? Am I living in obedience to God? Did that really just happen? What about those words she spoke over me?*

Then came the truth: *She has no hold on me! I belong to Jesus Christ.*

When I arrived home from the confrontation, Steve and I sat down together with our special family Bible that was given to us by our dear Grandpa Leo, an adopted grandpa who has been a spiritual mentor for us through the last three years. We experienced deep, joyful strength from the truth of God's Word. These verses from Psalm 62 are wonderful to meditate on, having the power to fill our entire beings with true rest of soul as the Creator's love brings healing to our hurts and freedom from our questions:

I am at rest in God alone; my salvation comes from Him.
He alone is my rock and my salvation, my stronghold; I will never be shaken.

How long will you threaten a man? Will all of you attack as if he were a leaning wall or a tottering stone fence? They only plan to bring him down from his high position. They take pleasure in lying; they bless with their mouths, but they curse inwardly. *Selah*

Rest in God alone, my soul, for my hope comes from Him. He alone is my rock and my salvation, my stronghold; I will not be shaken. My salvation and glory depend on God, my strong rock. My refuge is in God. Trust in Him at all times, you people; pour out your hearts before Him. God is our refuge. *Selah*

Men are only a vapor; exalted men, an illusion. Weighed in the scales, they go up; together they are less than a vapor. Place no trust in oppression, or false hope in robbery. If wealth increases, pay no attention to it.

God has spoken once; I have heard this twice: strength belongs to God, and faithful love belongs to You, LORD. For You repay each according to his works. (Ps. 62, HCSB)

DECLARING THE TRUTH: WE ARE LOVED!

Beyond our need to recognize the Spirit's voice regarding false teaching, we also need the Spirit's help to discern lies and wrong thinking that set up camp within us. We are attacked on multiple fronts: by the enemy, our own inner critics, our sin natures, and the influence of our culture. We are bombarded on a daily basis with information that needs to be sifted for truth.

In my morning communion one summer day, I was meditating on John 16 and at verse 27, I read, "I am dearly loved by my Father." This is truth. Any voice declaring that we are unloved, unwanted, or abandoned is *not* God's voice.

Besides the lies that we are unwanted or unloved, when hardship stretches on like miles and miles of bad road with no end in sight, we may also start hearing, "No one cares," "No one understands," "You're all alone," or "No one has time for you." Being grounded in God's Word reveals these pain-filled words to be lies. God *does* care: "Give all your worries and cares to God, for he cares about you" (1 Pet. 5:7). We are *never* alone: "I am with you always, even to the end of the age" (Matt. 28:20).

During my hardest days, I take a few minutes to read off my prayer wall a list of truths about who I am in Christ and about who Jesus is. I especially delight in raising my hands up to my Father and declaring out loud, "I am loved! Jesus *is* present, always willing and able to help."

DECLARING THE TRUTH: WE ARE NOT CONDEMNED!

"There is *no* condemnation for those who belong to Christ Jesus" (Rom. 8:1)! Voices in our heads constantly put us on trial. Sometimes we experience shame, guilt, and regret. But the voice of condemnation is never from God. We have an accuser, Satan, and he is going to have to answer to God for his accusations (see Rev. 12:10).

In John 7:53–8:11, we read about a woman being accused. Jesus responded to these accusations by bending down to draw in the dirt. I once heard a pastor present the idea that perhaps Jesus was writing in the dirt each of the sins of the Pharisees and scribes gathered around this woman, starting with the oldest one, because of course he had the most sin! Upon seeing their sins written down by Jesus, who knows *all* things, they left one by one. Soon it was just the woman and Jesus, and He said to her, "Neither do I condemn you. Go and sin no more" (see John 8:11). Jesus does not condemn. He does not shame us or make us feel guilty. Voice recognition has to do with knowing the truth of God's Word and depending on the Spirit to help us discern what is coming from our inner critics, what is coming from the enemy, and what is the gentle voice of Jesus.

I love how Jesus says, "Go and sin no more," because that's what love does. The love Jesus demonstrated on the cross set us free *from* sin, not *to* sin. When we taste His love, we lose our desire for sin and the ick it brings. So much pain comes from such short moments of fleeting pleasure. It's *not* worth it! As children of God, we will experience gentle conviction as the Lord's kindness leads us to repentance (see Rom. 2:4). The difference between condemnation and conviction is looking for that kindness that leads us to repentance, not being shamed into repentance. One brings despair; the other awakens hope. The Spirit within us, using the Word of God, will shine a light on the areas of our hearts where the enemy has set up camp. He will increase our desire to be clean. "Create in me a clean heart, O God, and renew a right spirit within me" (Ps. 51:10, ESV).

A big difference between condemnation and conviction is that when the Spirit points out things that need to change, He brings about a way for us to make that change! Condemnation is an endless cycle of lies; conviction is a path to renewal and a move toward holiness. "Your word is very pure; therefore Your servant loves it" (Ps. 119:140, NKJV).

Recognizing Past Whispers

The Spirit teaches us about Jesus and our Father. The Spirit awakens us to the beauty and work of Jesus Christ (see John 16:13–15). Anytime I have felt comfort, new strength, or learned something from the Bible, it was the work of the Spirit. Knowing that this is how the Spirit works, we can look back over our past years as God's children and remember moments when the Spirit powerfully comforted us, changed our plans for a day with His divine appointments, or clearly guided us through mazes of decisions with His Whisper "*This is the way; walk in it*" (Isa. 30:21, NIV).

One night, in my junior year of high school, I struggled to fall asleep. After midnight I finally realized that it was the Holy Spirit keeping me awake, and then I had a Samuel moment: "Okay, Jesus, speak, for I'm ready to listen." I got up out of bed to retrieve an unopened letter from a college in Oregon that I had thrown away earlier that day. I'd had *no* intention of leaving my family to go one thousand miles away to college! God, however, planned for me to go. A year and a half later, my parents left me, a crying seventeen-year-old freshman, at college in Salem, Oregon. (Thank you for your courage, Momma and Daddy, not to listen to me as I begged you not to leave me!) As it turned out, I *loved* not only my school but also the beautiful Northwest, where I reside today.

That still, small voice has been with me since I asked Jesus into my heart as a young child. The Spirit protected, guided, and loved me through leaving home as a seventeen-year-old, and He was with me in my hospital room when I was admitted for cancer testing, resulting in a diagnosis as a thirty-five-year-old. God is with me. God is with you. Always.

WALKING WITH JESUS

Snuggling with my kids at bedtime is one of my favorite parts of motherhood. One night I was with seven-year-old Gracie, who was praying that she would love Jesus with all her heart and walk with Him always. After I had finished praying, in her sweet voice, she said, "Momma, I was wondering something. How can I walk with Jesus if I can't see Him?"

Good question, Gracie! That sure made me think. How *should* I explain that to my young daughter?

We talked about how Jesus speaks to us in the Bible and about the Holy Spirit. I told Gracie that the best way for us to walk with

Jesus was to get to know Him so that we can recognize His voice when He is prompting us to do something, say something, or repent of something. We talked about how sometimes He just wants to let us know that He's with us and that He loves us. Walking with Jesus means staying in step with Him. It means going when He says, "Go," and resting when He says, "Rest." Gracie, as she so often does, smiled her happy, contented smile at me before saying her usual, "Goodnight, Momma. Have a good sleep. You're the best momma in the world!" I'm so glad Jesus gave me a Gracie!

In answering her question that night, I got to thinking about the moments I have made the Spirit sad by running ahead of Him. I was reminded to practice the power of the pause when uncertainty hits—especially when fear sets in, which tends to put our feet into fast-forward movement, resulting in exhaustion, confusion, and chaos. When we walk with Jesus, we will not make His Spirit sad by how we live (see Eph. 4:30). We will live as free children of God. Free *from* sin. Not free *to* sin. We will spend ample time in His Word because of our love and desire for the *only* peace—peace with God Himself, which satisfies our longing for all to be right in our world.

HIS VOICE IS GRACE

Grace will always have the last word for all of us who know Jesus. We must let that voice be the truth over our lives. Yes, we will mess up. Daily. But grace doesn't run out. We have the power to choose to step toward lies or truth with each thought we give permission to reside in our minds. We are loved. We are holy. We are forgiven. We are free. Recognizing our Savior's gentle voice of truth brings peace, joy, and victory. Jesus looks into our eyes, and we meet love of the truest kind. He is ours. We are His. Our souls find rest in our Creator's love through the gentle Whisper of truth within.

～ *Pray It In* ～

Father, You alone are God (see Ps. 86:10). Cause me to know, love, and use Your Word. Teach me to test everything, holding fast to what is good (see 1 Thess. 5:21). As I hide Your Word in my heart, grant me Your wisdom, protection, and freedom (see Ps. 119:11).

Jesus, thank You for taking hold of me today. I rest in Your love.

6

CHECKING THE
MUTE BUTTON

Steve and I met on my fourteenth birthday at a small Christian high school in Huntington Beach, California. During our close friendship in high school, we dated for a short time. I vividly remember Steve picking me up, in his family's minivan, for our first date. After he chivalrously helped me in on the passenger side, he gave old Betsy's headlight a solid whack before climbing into the driver's seat so it would turn on. My growing giggle burst into loud laughter when he also gave the radio a thump to help it turn on too!

Fast forward twenty-seven years, and we still periodically try the whack-it method for things that aren't working quite right. The other day I asked Steve if there was anything he could do for the flickering ceiling lights in our walk-in closet, also known as my prayer room. Sure enough, his tall six-foot-five self reached up, gently whacked the light, and—voila!—all fixed!

When it comes to audio issues with our tablets or laptops, rather than giving them a whack, we first check the mute button.

Most of the time the video has been muted, and a simple click fixes it! A similar problem, if it's with one of the kids' music players, is that the audio cord isn't always pushed in all the way.

Sometimes in our journeys with Jesus, His voice grows dim. This is our signal to be sure that the mute button is off and the audio cord is firmly connected.

MUTE BUTTON CHECK: THE CHURNING OF AN UN-SURRENDERED SOUL

I smile now thinking of my sweet Ellie Joy, who shares my sensitivity of soul. If she is feeling overwhelmed, anxious, or frustrated, hugs are the best choice rather than a lengthy exhortation. When calm has returned, she is able to receive encouragement and instruction. Parenting my four children gives me daily opportunities to learn about my relationship with my heavenly Father. Sometimes when I can't hear His voice, His Spirit has later shown me that it was due to my losing His Whisper in the deafening churn of my un-surrendered soul.

"Our soul is like an inner stream of water, which gives strength, direction, and harmony to every other element of life. When that stream is as it should be, we are constantly refreshed and exuberant in all we do, because our soul itself is then rooted in the vastness of God and His kingdom!"[1] In order to hear the Whisper within, my experiences have taught me that the two most important steps are to live in obedience to all God asks of us and to be fully dependent on God alone, always.

Obedience, even when He has asked me to follow uncharted waters and defy man's wisdom, has restored the melody of His Whisper within me numerous times! The Spirit in us is brave and eager to do the will of the Father. Our choice to obey and live in full dependence on God results in living lives in consistent conversation with our Savior. As we center our thoughts on His greatness and goodness, we will experience a gentle flow of peace through the indwelling Spirit.

MUTE BUTTON CHECK: THANKFUL SOUL EYES

"Let not thy mind run on what thou lackest, as much as on what thou hast already."[2] Thankfulness sensitizes us to God's voice and restores our vision when it has become cloudy.

When we are distanced from the Father's voice, it helps to start listing all our blessings—every single thing that comes to mind when we consider what we are thankful for. For me, that could be from the breath I just took to the rainbow during a drive through Portland's city traffic. It could be from a giggle that came during a crushing disappointment to my seven-year-old son's signature wraparound hug, which he gives by asking me to sit down so he can attach himself like a koala bear around me and squeeze as tightly as he can. Sometimes it is bringing a sacrifice of praise, which tunes my ear to the right frequency to hear Him speak.

The eye is the lamp of the body. If our eyes are healthy, then our whole bodies will be full of light (see Matt. 6:22). For healthy vision, let us fasten our eyes to the cross, where Jesus demonstrated His love for us in that while we were yet sinners, He died for us (see Rom. 5:8). In considering the life, death, and resurrection of the Son of God, our thoughts become centered on our deliverance from the kingdom of darkness and our entrance into the kingdom of light. The cross reminds us of the magnitude of our heavenly Father's love—love being the essence of God's triune being as God our Father, God the Son, and God the Holy Spirit. They invite us into Their perfect eternal love relationship.

How can it be? We are loved with the love that the Father has for the Son (see John 17:26)! For this I am daily and eternally grateful. Through thankful soul eyes, light fills our entire beings.

MUTE BUTTON CHECK: DARK CORNERS

During one of my spiritual fasts, I asked Jesus to shine a light on any dark corners of sin or unbelief in my heart that needed His cleansing. The Lord searches our innermost beings, exposing every hidden motive (see Prov. 20:27). Sin has a weakening effect. Our minds are quick to quantify sins as big sins or little sins. But all sin devastates and debilitates, whether it's pride, envy, self-indulgences, unforgiveness, selfishness, anger, deceit, or poisonous roots of bitterness (see Heb. 12:15). There is no little sin; all sins have a large impact. When we choose to go our own way, we lose God's strength at work within us. Sin dulls our capacity to hear the Whisper within.

Luke 11:34 speaks of being singularly focused. We will be changed by what we draw near to. Our choices step us toward darkness or toward light. Our words, our actions, how we spend time, what we choose to read or watch—it all affects who we become.

As we spend more time with Jesus, we will become more aware of His intense love for us, and our love for Him will deepen. This love pulls us away from our own wills and into His. As we step back onto His chosen path for our lives, light increases with each prayer of repentance. Repentance—turning from sin and going God's way—is beautiful! Repentance brings refreshment! "Repent of your sins and turn to God, so that your sins may be wiped away. Then times of refreshment will come from the presence of the Lord, and he will again send you Jesus, your appointed Messiah" (Acts 3:19–20). This refreshment brings peace! The world cannot give us peace, but being in right relationship with God can—and does.

Not all seasons of darkness are brought about by our sin, but all seasons of darkness warrant running to the light of Jesus and asking Him to speak into the darkness. Recently I shared with Steve that I felt like a dried-up crumbly well. People kept asking me for things, but I had nothing to give.

The word "cistern" kept coming to me. I remembered from a past Bible study something about a broken cistern. I was delivered from that particular night season when God shone a light on the words of Jeremiah the prophet to give me the picture of a broken cistern and my need to return to the fountain of living waters. "My people have done two evil things: They have abandoned me—the fountain of living water. And they have dug for themselves cracked cisterns that can hold no water at all" (Jer. 2:13)!

I used my Bible dictionary to read the description of a cistern and found myself a perfect match! A cistern was used to hold rainwater during the months of rain to supply for dry seasons. I felt crumbly, with no capacity to continue pouring out to others following a season of busyness. I had spent less time alone with Jesus than usual, less time drinking from His pure, freely flowing living water to receive everything I needed for my days.

My awareness of His bright presence and clear voice within me has often been restored when I have fervently asked Jesus to expose any dark corners and sweep them clean, filling each one with more of Himself. In Psalm 51, David recognized his sin and cried out to God. It is a wonderful passage of Scripture to turn to in times when we cannot hear our Lord's voice.

Reading and praying these passages from Psalm 51 as we envision ourselves in our Father's arms, held snugly in the safety of His love and endless mercy, will bring us back into His presence:

Have mercy upon me, O God, according to Your loving-kindness; according to the multitude of Your tender mercies, blot out my transgressions. Wash me thoroughly from my iniquity, and cleanse me from my sin. For I acknowledge my transgressions, and my sin is always before me. (Ps. 51:1–3, NKJV)

Create in me a pure heart, O God, and renew a steadfast spirit within me. Do not cast me from your presence or take your Holy Spirit from me. Restore to me the joy of your salvation and grant me a willing spirit, to sustain me. (Ps. 51:10–12, NIV)

As we are restored to intimate fellowship with Him, let's refuse to choose our feelings over His Word. When we confess our sin, He is faithful and just and forgives our sin and cleanses us from all unrighteousness (see 1 John 1:9). It is truly our most painful loss when we lose even one ounce of the fullness of the Spirit because we allow sin to make its home in some dark corner of our hearts. Praise be to God for His forgiveness, for the blood of the Lamb! That is how we will overcome—because *He* overcame.

AUDIO CORD CONNECTION: SITTING LONG WITH THE WRITTEN VOICE

Seasons of silence are a call for us to linger long in solitude with the Lord's written voice, His Word, where we can always hear Him, even when our connection to the Spirit has grown dim. "It is when the soul is hushed in silent awe and worship before the Holy Presence that reveals itself within, that the still small voice of the blessed Spirit will be heard."[3]

Jesus, the Word, is our light: "In the beginning was the Word, and the Word was with God, and the Word was God. He was in the beginning with God. All things were made through him, and without him was not anything made that was made. In him was life, and the life was the light of men. The light shines in the darkness, and the darkness has not overcome it" (John 1:1–5,

ESV). We can come to Jesus in stillness of soul and ask Him to search us and know our hearts, to try us and know our thoughts, to see if there is any way in us that grieves Him, and to lead us in the way everlasting (see Ps. 139:23–24).

When we return to meditating on God's Word day and night, it can brighten a dark night. His Word is a lamp unto our feet and a light unto our paths (see Ps. 119:105). When darkness troubles our souls, we can slow our schedules and our minds. We can hover close to His Word, spending more time reading it, or listening to it on audio if reading under the heavy weight of night feels too difficult. When we come upon a section that speaks to us, we can camp out by its warmth, recognizing the Spirit's presence as He illuminates words of comfort.

The Word is the answer to our culture's increasing demands that are decreasing our awareness of our heavenly Father's presence and power in our lives as His children. Through His written voice, God has frequently revealed shadows over my soul that were created by habitual sins that dimmed the reality of His presence in me. As that reality dwindled, I began to believe the lies of the enemy taunting me that I was unloved and forgotten. When we listen to the voice of accusation, chaos increases and peace decreases. Jesus is our peace, and sitting long with His written voice will scatter the lies and return us to a place of quiet.

SEASONS OF WAITING

Sometimes God plops us down in waiting rooms. I have known both joy and sorrow in waiting-room experiences during my cancer journey: physically as I came face to face with a sea of suffering and spiritually while waiting on Jesus—waiting for Him to *do* something, to change, to restore, to simply fix what I could not fix.

This world is in need of much fixing. Do you feel that? Has it increased for you too? The multiplying needs. The pain walking the streets. The heaviness of hearts. Even within the walls of my own home, numerous needs have been raised up in prayer that are awaiting His response.

At times I have confused seasons of silence or darkness with divinely allowed seasons of waiting as God has worked quietly, beyond the curtain of my earthly vision. At times I wrongly assume that God is *not* working or speaking simply because He has asked me to wait on Him. The mute button is off—I am truly listening for His voice. But He is simply asking me to wait— to wait long; to wait with trust, even if I have to tremble a bit; to do what He has shown me that I *can* do as I wait; to take the next visible step while trusting His perfectly timed unveiling of moments to come.

> Show me Your ways, O LORD; teach me Your paths. Lead me in Your truth and teach me, for You are the God of my salvation; on You I wait all the day. (Ps. 25:4–5, NKJV)

Oh, that we may wait quietly before God, for our hope is in Him (see Ps. 62:5)! The result of fully waiting on God is a life of victory in Jesus. It's a peace that is ever present, because Jesus Himself is our peace. He guaranteed us not lives without bumps but that He would never leave us. Jesus is the reason we can wait in a position of soul rest and childlike faith, trusting our perfect parent to supply all we need at the proper time.

SEASONS OF NIGHT

We long for the joy that comes in the morning, but our night hours seem to drag on. We open our hands in surrender. We ask the Spirit to reveal any dark corners in our souls. We choose thankfulness. We sit long with the written voice of God, turning page after page, longing for His voice to boom out at any moment. We accept that we are in seasons of waiting. But darkness hovers, and silence stays. Then what?

During a particularly hard stretch this last summer, my soul was stuck in night, despite the long sunny days. I tried my best to trust, thank, and praise, but my time in the closet felt more like a discipline than a joy. I began to beg Jesus for a "word from His Word," which has become my habitual practice when the heat of hard times increases, when I am restless in my waiting, or when doubt creeps in about His promises to me. I simply cry out to our great shepherd, who cares tenderly for His sheep, "A word, Lord; please, a word!" God's Word is what we are to stand upon, not our feelings. If our faith was built on our emotions or on good news, we would be cyclical messes. Jesus is the rock upon which our souls can stand, even in the night seasons.

If we were stuck in a dark room, we wouldn't sprint around the room looking for the light switch. We would feel for the wall and proceed alongside it with caution. Similarly, most of us would not run a 5K race in the middle of the night! Darkness is not designed for running. When our souls experience seasons of night, we need to slow down and draw near to God, and He will draw near to us (see James 4:8).

If we look intensely for a word from His Word to hold fast to during the night, joy *will* come again. We can return to Him once again through the steps outlined in the previous five chapters of this book: We start by creating quiet spaces and spending hours in communion with the One whose understanding is *infinite* (see Ps. 147:5). We then remove our shoes and bow in reverence before our Creator. We were by nature children of wrath, deserving of eternal punishment, but thanks be to God, who saved us from His wrath through the blood of His Son! Oh, how rich is His mercy (see Eph. 2:3–5)! Next we visit the Isaac altar, placing all that we hold dear on top and emptying our hands. We turn our palms down in wholehearted surrender to our God, who gives and takes away, blessed be His name (see Job 1:21)! Then we earnestly ask for the darkness to lift through fasting. Finally, we ask Him to increase our recognition of *His* voice and to help us tune out the lies that tend to increase in our seasons of darkness.

During my night season this past summer, I earnestly prayed that our Father would give me a specific tangible reminder of His love for me. He answered! I was taking a walk, and on the path in front of me, someone had written "YOU ARE LOVED" in sidewalk chalk in huge letters. True story! Later that afternoon, when I was fixing a cup of tea, I noticed a perfectly beautiful heart design in the granite countertop that I had never noticed before. I can't help but smile when I am heating water or cleaning the countertops these days; that heart is perfectly placed for me to notice in my daily rhythms.

In my darkest hours, I cannot sense God's presence. Every thought is a battle. Our instinct is to turn away from people when we need them most, but reaching out to just one trusted friend in a time of darkness lightens our pain. When we cannot muster up a prayer, they can lay hands on us and pray in the Spirit over us.

God can also use our night experiences to help us be present as His tangible love to others. God doesn't have the limitations, weariness, and seasons of discouragement that we do, but those in our forever families all experience seasons of night. Sometimes the best gift we can give our brothers and sisters is our love without any expectations. Jesus teaches us, "Freely you have received, so freely give" (see Matt. 10:8).

We can continue in reverence for God, even from our helpless places. Nothing honors Him more than when we lay down like children in complete trust at His feet, believing that He is all we need and that He will move on our behalf. Reverence for God is when we remind ourselves of who *He* is: His power, His infiniteness in every character trait. He is infinitely full of energy, infinitely merciful, and infinitely powerful.

When His voice within me feels faint and His presence less real, I first sit under His searchlight and ask Him to scan my soul for un-surrendered pockets in need of His Savior love; perhaps I have started down the road of doing things my own way after growing tired of waiting. Next I bring the sacrifice of praise and thanksgiving, reminding my soul of who God is and how faithful He has been to me. I ask the Spirit to reveal any dark corners of sin or unbelief that have set up house in my innermost being. I sit long with His written voice, which strengthens my soul during the waiting-room and night seasons I encounter. I gaze upon the cross, fixing the eyes of my soul upon the place where He demonstrated His love for me in that while I was a sinner, He died for me (see Rom. 5:8). As His love runs red down the cross, over me, His Whisper within reminds me that I am His and He is mine. My soul is quieted and held as I rest there in my Creator's love.

Pray It In

Adonai, You hear the desires of the meek (see Ps. 10:17). You shine in my darkness (see Ps. 18:28). You promised Your people who are called by Your name that if we humble ourselves and pray, and turn from our wicked ways, You will hear from heaven, forgive our sins, and heal our lands (see 2 Chron. 7:14). Protect my soul from sin that clouds my view of Your love. Teach me to come to You hour by hour, to surrender all of myself into Your love (see Matt. 11:28). I ask fervently, and I confidently wait on You as I ask (see Ps. 27:14).

Jesus, thank You for taking hold of me today. I rest in Your love.

PART 2

WHAT WHISPERS DO

7

WHISPERS
SILENCE FEAR

One summer weekend in July after our family moved back to the Portland area, Steve took Luke on his first camping trip in Oregon. They chose Elk Creek campground in the Tillamook National Forest, a first-come, first-served campground. As Steve was leaving home, I told him that once he let me know that they had arrived safely and were able to secure a spot, I wouldn't expect to hear a peep from them until they returned home.

I regretted those words with increasing fervor when hour after hour passed by without hearing from them. Thanks to Google Maps location sharing, I am used to being able to see where Steve is every few minutes when his phone updates his location. Anxiety took root when I noticed that the last time his phone had checked in was miles from where they should have been. I tried calling and texting over and over. I started worrying about Steve and Luke having been in a car wreck and considered driving out there to check!

After an hour of restless turmoil, I cried out to Jesus for peace. The Lord answered through His Whisper within, "*Trust Me, not your phone!*"

Sometimes the truth is a bit painful. I had been suffering from misplaced trust syndrome, choosing to trust a small rectangular manmade device over the Almighty. Something beautiful happened late in the afternoon on that July summer day. The Holy Spirit turned the key to the lock on the handcuffs chaining me to my phone, drawing me to Himself—and fear left. Fear fogs our vision and has a freezing effect on us, stopping us from moving forward into our days and our lives. Praise be to Jesus! I put my phone away, feeling affirmation that our heavenly Father was watching over Steve and Luke. I returned my focus to my younger three children waiting patiently by my side, and we proceeded to have a good weekend.

All was well with Steve and Luke. They had unexpectedly lost cell-phone reception miles before they arrived at the campground. They returned home with radiant smiles and two days' worth of adventures to share with me. I love listening to Luke share about his experiences because he is able to remember vivid details and describe them in a way that draws me deep into his experiences. I was thankful that Jesus had rescued me from fear while they were away so I could fully delight in hearing about their time together.

The first half of this book took us through steps of preparation to hear God's voice. The second half will turn our focus toward the effect that the Spirit's Whisper has on the life of a Christ follower. In the next six chapters, I will highlight a few of the ways God's Word and God's Spirit have moved me into resting in His love as He has shaped me a bit more, degree by degree, into the image of Jesus (see 2 Cor. 3:18). The Whisper to trust Jesus and not to fear is one example of the many ways His Whisper has restored my soul to rest in His love.

LOVE SILENCES FEAR

I tasted cold dark fear in 2013. The doctor's words "We think you have cancer" bounced around the white hospital walls alongside my growing "what if" questions bouncing around my head. "What if I die?" "What if Steve is left to raise our four young children alone?" "What if my children have to grow up without me?" Sometimes we get so caught up in the "what ifs" that we lose sight of what *is* and who *God* is, the King of the universe ruling everything and everyone in it. He is love Himself, our safe place. He fills us with songs of deliverance when we lean into Him with childlike trust: "You are my hiding place; you will protect me from trouble and surround me with songs of deliverance" (Ps. 32:7, NIV).

While we are to fear God with reverential fear (see chapter 2), there is a type of fear that is never from God. The most repetitive command in all of Scripture is "Do not fear," because the Lord knows that we are prone to the fear of man and of circumstances. God's Word reminds us that *He* is love (see 1 John 4:8). Not only that, "there is no fear in love. But perfect love drives out fear, because fear has to do with punishment. The one who fears is not made perfect in love" (1 John 4:18, NIV).

When we experience fear during affliction, it is an invitation for us to draw near to Jesus. "In the storm, the tree strikes deeper roots in the soil; in the hurricane the inhabitants of the house abide within, and rejoice in its shelter. So by suffering the Father would have us enter more deeply into the love of Christ."[1] As we settle deeper into our shepherd's arms, His Whisper of love from within silences the fear knocking on our hearts' doors.

THINKING ON JESUS

Training our brains to think much on Jesus protects our minds from being hijacked by fear. Instead of battling fear on our own, we must pick up the sword of the Spirit and let Jesus fight for us. Speaking affirmations of truth from God's Word strips fear of any power over us as God's children.

Speaking the Word of God has helped me find firm ground when anxiety is taking me out to sea. Anxiety, a manifestation of fear, can show up in the human body in ways unique to each person. Whenever I am waiting to hear test results for cancer, my heart speeds up and pounds loud and hard. Anxiety can be debilitating. Our tender shepherd provides safety within the green pastures of His Word.

Here are some of the affirmations of truth we can speak when fear visits:

You are the God who carries me. (see Deut. 1:31)

You are with me. You are my God. You will strengthen me. You will help me. You will uphold me with Your victorious right hand. (see Isa. 41:10)

When I go through deep waters, You are with me. When I go through rivers of difficulty, I will not drown. When I walk through the fire of oppression, I will not be burned up; the flames will not consume me. (see Isa. 43:2)

I am precious to You. (see Isa. 43:4)

You love me. (see Isa. 43:4)

You are with me always, to the very end of the age. (see Matt. 28:20)

I give my burdens to You. You take care of me. You will not let me slip and fall. (see Ps. 55:22)

My life and my breath are in Your hand. (see Job 12:10)

As I listen to You, I will live in peace, untroubled by fear of harm. (see Prov. 1:33)

My strength will equal my days. (see Deut. 33:25)

This battle belongs to You, Lord. (see 2 Chron. 20:15)

You go before me and follow me. You place Your hand of blessing on my head. (see Ps. 139:5)

I know that my fears for today and worries for tomorrow will not separate me from Your love. (see Rom. 8:38)

You gave me the gift of a peaceful mind and heart. (see John 14:27)

You will personally go ahead of me. You will neither fail nor abandon me. (see Deut. 31:6)

Your perfect love drives out fear. (see 1 John 4:18)

You answer me. You free me from all my fears. (see Ps. 34:4)

You are my refuge and strength. You are always ready to help in times of trouble. (see Ps. 46:1)

Sometimes fear comes when life begins to spiral out of our control. Yet in Psalm 29, we are reminded that "the LORD rules over the floodwaters. The LORD reigns as king forever" (Ps. 29:10). Our King was reigning over the flood in Noah's day, and He sits as Lord over our circumstances today!

There is a God-appointed limit to any hardship we are allowed to endure. "Who kept the sea inside its boundaries as it burst from the womb, and as I clothed it with clouds and wrapped it in thick darkness? For I locked it behind barred gates, limiting its shores. I said, 'This far and no farther will you come. Here your proud waves must stop!'" (Job 38:8–11). Just as God set limits to the seas, He has set divine boundaries on any trial and period of testing we are allowed to face.

God's Word contains checks ready to be cashed. He is who He says He is. He will do what He says He will do. All we need to do is *receive* the Word. Trusting His Savior signature on the countless promises found in God's Word is what anchors us when we encounter the wind and waves here on Earth. God gives strength to His people; He blesses His people with peace (see Ps. 29:11). This is His promise to us, a check to be cashed by praying, "Father, I receive these words into my entire being. I receive Your peace. I receive Your strength."

CHOOSING TO SING

On a visit to my sister Lynnette in Southern California, a Christian radio station was playing in the car while she and I enjoyed conversation together. My mind and heart were weighed down by ache—an ache that comes to me when life is hard for those I love and I cannot fix it, or that settles in me when worries creep in and fear tries to make its home within my soul. Suddenly we heard my darling five-year-old niece, Luna, begin to praise Jesus from the back seat as she passionately sang along with the radio. Jesus knew that I needed Luna to belt out the truth of who Jesus was when my heart felt too heavy to sing. Oh, how beautiful is the faith of a child!

When sighing or sorrow has stolen our voices, we can raise a hand to the sky, pointing up to Jesus as the King over all. When facing darkness, in the midst of questions, we can gain the help of a fellow comrade of the cross. Our forever family, the body of Christ, can speak the name of Jesus over our hearts and our homes.

Roaring King Jesus will be returning for us. He came like a lamb, and He will return as a lion. Darkness will leave forever. Today He is our light. His name is victory. He rides across the heavens to help us, across the skies in majestic splendor. The eternal God is our refuge, and His everlasting arms are under us (see Deut. 33:26–27).

JESUS OUR RESCUE

I am drawn to the apostle Peter's bold and passionate heart. When Peter saw Jesus walking on the water in the midst of the storm, he called out in honesty,

> "Lord, if it's really you, tell me to come to you, walking on the water."
> "Yes, come," Jesus said.

So Peter went over the side of the boat and walked on the water toward Jesus. But when he saw the strong wind and the waves, he was terrified and began to sink. "Save me, Lord!" he shouted.

Jesus immediately reached out and grabbed him. "You have so little faith," Jesus said. "Why did you doubt me?" (Matt. 14:28–31)

Before we think too long on Peter's failure to keep his eyes on Jesus, can we all give Peter some credit for getting *out* of the boat to begin with? Go, Peter! I can resonate with Peter's asking, "Is it *really* You, Lord?" Have you ever felt God nudging you to do something that felt extreme? Maybe to go against the accepted norm in Christian circles? To get out of your comfortable boat and step onto deep waters of faith? Peter obeyed Jesus when the Lord invited him to come.

Sometimes after our obedience, we expect an instant quieting of the storm. When the waves instead grow more boisterous, we are tempted to take our eyes off Jesus, and we lose awareness of His power at work within us. We see that we have no control over our circumstances and begin to sink as fear grabs hold. Peter cried out, "Save me, Lord!" Don't you love how Jesus *immediately* reached out His hand and saved Peter? The Lord hears our cries for help!

The LORD says, "I will rescue those who love me. I will protect those who trust in my name. When they call on me, I will answer; I will be with them in trouble. I will rescue and honor them. I will reward them with a long life and give them my salvation." (Ps. 91:14–16)

AN INTERCEDING SAVIOR

Amazing grace, how can it be? *Jesus* is praying for *me*?

It would be quite impossible for me to choose only *one* favorite chapter of the Bible. In the running for that blue ribbon would be John 17—imagine, the King of the universe, our Messiah, praying for us! Jesus prayed first that the faith of His disciples would not fail. He did not pray for them to be taken out of the world but to be protected from the evil one (see John 17:15). Then we too are included in the prayer of our most high priest: "I am praying not only for these disciples but also for all who will ever believe in me through their message" (John 17:20).

Rather than address fear with self-effort, we should remember that Jesus is praying over us. With childlike faith, we can sing, "Jesus *loves* me!" When we center our thoughts on Jesus, His greatness grows in us, while fear shrinks.

Choosing not to be debilitated, discouraged, or destroyed by fear has been a moment-by-moment experience for me. It has been almost seven years since the day of my cancer diagnosis. I've been in remission for four of those years, yet fear can still visit me. What we fear is not always in our today; sometimes it's in the mystery of tomorrow. "The future is not yet ours; perhaps it never will be. If it comes, it may come wholly different from what we have foreseen. Let us shut our eyes then to that which God hides from us, and keeps in reserve in the treasures of His deep counsels."[2]

I love to focus my mind on the truth that Jesus is praying for me, my *lion* who will be returning for me! My fear is lost in the sound of King Jesus' roaring protection over my life. The great I AM is present and powerful over my fear as His love continually floods through me.

Turn the Light Switch On

On New Year's Eve in 2019, our family of six gathered in my prayer closet. Once everyone had a spot, we turned the light off, plunging ourselves into complete darkness. The younger children did *not* like sitting in the darkness. Ellie Joy and Sammy J regularly express thankfulness that heaven will not include darkness.

My closet is ridiculously big, but when all six of us sat down on the floor, the closet space seemed to shrink. While sitting in the darkness, we talked about not being strong enough on our own to fight the darkness that visits our minds. The path to victory is to run to Jesus and His Word. We asked the children what happens when we turn on a light switch. Then I reached up and turned the light on in our closet. *Poof!* Darkness disappeared! We cannot think better or fight fear by trying harder. What does help is exercising our God-given power of choice to turn on the light switch of God's Word and speak the name of Jesus into our darkness.

We lit six candles, gave out cards with verses written on them to each one, and turned the light off once more. One by one the children spoke the light of God's Word into our minds and hearts. Sammy J read, "Blessed are the pure in heart, for they will see God" (Matt. 5:8, NIV). Next came Ellie Joy: "Your word is a lamp to guide my feet and a light for my path" (Ps. 119:105). Gracie declared, "Taste and see that the LORD is good. Oh, the joys of those who take refuge in him!" (Ps. 34:8). Steve's deep voice followed: "I am the light of the world. Whoever follows me will not walk in darkness, but will have the light of life" (John 8:12, ESV). Our firstborn, Luke, whose very name means "bringer of light," closed with, "You are the fountain of life, the light by which we see" (Ps. 36:9).

I went to each child, laying my hands on their heads, and prayed a prayer of blessing over them: that they would love and follow Jesus always, that their hearts would be guarded as the wellspring of their lives (see Prov. 4:23), and that they would be pure in heart and would see God (see Matt. 5:8). We prayed that as a family we would hide these verses in our hearts in 2020 and be the light of Jesus to a storm-darkened world.

PEACE BEGINS IN THE SOUL

In wellness of soul, peace grows. When our souls are calm and connected to the Spirit within us, the Spirit discharges Himself into every beat of our hearts, every thought in our minds, and every cell in our bodies. Our soul is the innermost part of our beings. It's what can hurt the most and also where the best cartwheels take place when joy abounds. When hurt feels heavy, we can "pray for grace to see in every trouble, small or great, the Father's finger pointing to Jesus, and saying, 'Abide in Him.'"[3]

When we cast the outcomes of painful circumstances onto our Father, knowing that we are not the ones who hold the power to make things turn out right, He answers by filling our souls with peace. This peace rises above our need to understand.

When I am overwhelmed, it helps me to take time alone in the quiet of my room to bring my thoughts Godward. If it's raining outside, I crack my window open to listen to God's music. In the summer, I may hear frogs or crickets. Sometimes I turn on cello hymn music. Other times silence suits me best. I light a candle to remind me of the light that Jesus is. After a few minutes, I lie down on my bedroom floor, spreading my arms in the cross position. Allowing the weight of my body to sink into the floor, I feel my muscles release my worries. I ask my perfect parent above to father my soul, placing His hands on my head, absorbing my questions with His clear Whispers of love. Sometimes the Spirit brings scriptures to my mind that I should pray. I tell Him everything. I remember the faithfulness of my Father who called me into fellowship with His Son, Jesus Christ my Lord (see 1 Cor. 1:9). I begin to thank Jesus for taking my place on the cross, for carrying the burdens that have caused unrest in my day.

Meditating on who Jesus *is* and on His perfect love that was demonstrated on the cross sets us free from the talons of fear. As I release all of me into all of Him, His love provides an escape from anxiety as I ask Him to move out my fear with His love. Fear is fleeting, but love is forever!

The "mind over matter" approach to fear has never worked for me. Rather than thinking harder to make it stop, meditating on scriptures that point me to God's love brings calm over me. Psalm 34 is a wonderful place to go for Scripture meditation when fear interrupts the flow of peace within me:

I will praise the LORD at all times. I will constantly speak his praises. I will boast only in the LORD; let all who are helpless take heart. Come, let us tell of the LORD's greatness; let us exalt his name together.

I prayed to the LORD, and he answered me. He freed me from all my fears. Those who look to him for help will be radiant with joy; no shadow of shame will darken their faces. In my desperation I prayed, and the LORD listened; he saved me from all my troubles. For the angel of the LORD is a guard; he surrounds and defends all who fear him.

Taste and see that the LORD is good. Oh, the joys of those who take refuge in him! Fear the LORD, you his godly people, for those who fear him will have all they need. Even strong young lions sometimes go hungry, but those who trust in the LORD will lack no good thing.

Come, my children, and listen to me, and I will teach you to fear the LORD. Does anyone want to live a life that is long and prosperous? Then keep your tongue from speaking evil and your lips from telling lies! Turn away from evil and do good. Search for peace, and work to maintain it.

The eyes of the LORD watch over those who do right; his ears are open to their cries for help. But the LORD turns his face against those who do evil; he will erase their memory from the earth. The LORD hears his people when they call to him for help. He rescues them from all their troubles. The LORD is close to the brokenhearted; he rescues those whose spirits are crushed.

The righteous person faces many troubles, but the LORD comes to the rescue each time. For the LORD protects the bones of the righteous; not one of them is broken!

Calamity will surely destroy the wicked, and those who hate the righteous will be punished. But the LORD will redeem those who serve him. No one who takes refuge in him will be condemned.

I experienced what the safety of drawing near to Jesus felt like one afternoon as I entered the mega tent that my kids had built in their play area upstairs. They had created five separate rooms, including three bedrooms, from sheets, chairs, and clothespins. I crawled into each child's room to join in their delight as each expressed how safe he or she felt inside the little tent rooms. This is like the place of safety offered to us when we draw near to the heart of our Father. Our souls find rest as our fear is silenced through the Whispers of His love within.

ꞏ Pray It In ꞏ

In my distress I call on You, Adonai. Set me high upon a rock (see Ps. 27:5).

I cry to You for help. You hear my voice. My cry comes into your ears. You are my rock, my fortress, and my deliverer. I take refuge in You. You are my shield and my stronghold. You reach down from on high and take hold of me. You draw me out of mighty waters (see Ps. 18:3, 7, 17). Adonai, You set the boundaries for the sea so that the waters never transgress Your command (see Prov. 8:29). When I am in awe of You, when I fear You, I will lack no good thing (see Ps. 34:10). Your angel encamps all around me (see Ps. 34:7). Holy Spirit, cause Your peace to circulate through my heart, mind, will, and body today. You are love. You are hope. You are my peace. You are within me. Discharge Yourself throughout my veins.

Jesus, thank You for taking hold of me today. I rest in Your love.

8

WHISPERS
PURIFY DESIRES

Aherd of thoughts began their morning stampede through my groggy mind as my tired eyes slowly opened. New challenges and concerns had kept Steve and me up talking late into the night. Going to bed without an "I surrender all to Jesus" appointment had resulted in a restless night followed by the morning parade of worries spoiling the fresh start to my day. Waking up to pounding thoughts is evidence of a troubled soul in need of time alone with Jesus to renew our awareness of His presence and once again lay down our desires before Him.

We trust Jesus. We surrender all to Him. We declare these truths as wholehearted followers of Jesus Christ—but they are tested when trials hit like tornadoes and stir up the angst within us that reveals our deepest desires. The winds of affliction rip off the outward cover of our self-confidence, exposing our vulnerable souls struggling with questions that rise up when life doesn't look like we hoped it would.

The Spirit's Whispers of love from within assure us that He is our highest good. We can once again lay down our every desire in total surrender to Him.

Oh, how glad I am that the Father never ever gives up on His children! Love is who God is, and He never changes. He simply can't stop loving us. His Spirit will continue to speak all that we need to hear, again and again, until our promotion day when we are richly welcomed into the kingdom (see 2 Pet. 1:11). I have often shared tearful giggles of self-exasperation with Jesus, declaring, "I'm so sorry, Lord!" I get frustrated with myself, but my Father is patient with His girl. He is awaiting His prodigal's return every time she wanders from wholehearted devotion to her King.

God's loving Whisper within me has held me when my desires have been thwarted and my troubles have grown strong. In parenting highly sensitive children, I have learned mostly by mistake that they aren't hearing me when they are frozen by fear, convulsed in sobs, or intensely expressing through words the unfairness of life. Once calm returns, the channel of communication can flow again. This is like the Spirit within us, inviting us to express ourselves the way our children do when they need an emotional release. He keeps us rooted in the love of our Father, looking into the tender gaze of Jesus, waiting patiently until we have released all our desires into all of Him.

When I awaken to a herd of elephant-sized anxious longings trampling my peace, I can choose to lie still a few minutes longer and turn my thoughts to Jesus. I can wait for those familiar Whispers of love to quiet the noise in my inner being, assuring me, "*Yes, My daughter, I am here. I am strong in you. I will keep telling you as often as you need to hear that I love you. I love you. I love you.*"

As we deeply connect with the Holy Spirit through our surrenders, His Whisper within purifies the desires of our hearts.

DESIRE TO TURN OUR FACES INTO THE WIND

Recently the pastor of our local church spoke on turning our faces toward our troubles rather than desiring easier lives. These words pierced my heart. I saw the last eight years of my life whiz by me on replay. How many times had I cried out for life to be easier? A sobering few minutes went by as I chewed on his words. Yes, I fully agreed. As believers, we should not desire our lives to be easier. The Spirit's gentle conviction melted me deep into my chair as I asked Jesus to forgive me.

As our pastor invited us to commit to a new way, I sat straight up and raised my hand. Yes! I joined others in choosing to turn our faces toward our troubles, trusting in the Father's love for us. I committed to press in, knowing that it is often the trials in our lives that open the door to God's favor.

In a world broken by sin, we will continue to face trials of all kinds. The desire to turn our faces into the wind and say, "I trust You, Father!" brings us into the peaceful eye of the storm. We leap with joy when the Spirit in us causes us to face our fears with courage because of His presence within us.

Our valleys of trouble become gateways of hope (see Hos. 2:15). Oh, how true that has been for me! I have been in the eye of cancer's storm. I have been brought through doorways of hope into my Father's favor, receiving blessing after blessing from the heavenly realms. Oh, for grace to trust Him more! For grace to look long upon Jesus, watching expectantly as I pray, "My voice You shall hear in the morning, O LORD; in the morning I will direct it to You, and I will look up" (Ps. 5:3, NKJV).

Jesus turned His face into the wind when He surrendered to His Father's will, looking past the cross to the joy beyond. The triune Godhead is inseparable in character and in will. The love of Jesus for His Father shone through His obedience, the Spirit within Him speaking and strengthening Him. When we turn to face the wind, we are following the footsteps of our Savior, turning to Him faces marked by surrender and trust, fixing our eyes on our heavenly Father.

DESIRE TO PERSEVERE

On my forty-first birthday, Steve and I were settled in our favorite spot by the fireplace in our living room, conversing about the way Jesus has upheld our family. We discussed how the enemy knows that when our flesh is attacked, we are more susceptible to turning from God than turning toward Him (see Job 2:4). But the Lord was *strong* in Job. God knew He would uphold Job's faith. And then my Whisper came: *"And I will be strong in you!"* My response came from my soul: "Lord, I will trust You with my pain." His words to me that night were to take a new grip, strengthen my knees, and mark out a straight path for my feet (see Heb. 12:12–13).

I believe deep in my bones, in my soul, and throughout my entire being that Jesus loves me. I am His beloved, and He is mine. This creates a burning desire in me to persevere and not grow weary of doing good, for in due season we will reap if we do not give up (see Gal. 6:9)! I choose to join the apostle Paul by taking a long view of temporary troubles. God's grace is reaching more and more people as His kingdom grows and His glory increases (see 2 Cor. 4:15–18).

It can be difficult to keep doing the right thing when we don't perceive that our efforts are accomplishing what we expected them to. But perhaps God's idea of what is being accomplished is different than ours. What if it has more to do with shaping our character than finding solutions to life's difficulties? Trusting His love helps us persevere through long and difficult circumstances. "We know how much God loves us, and we have put our trust in his love" (1 John 4:16). We will find new strength to persevere when we take the time to think of all the hostility Jesus endured so that we won't become weary and give up (see Heb. 12:3).

The Spirit shone a light for me on a passage in Deuteronomy to renew my desire to persevere in loving obedience to Jesus as I awaited His divinely appointed late rains in my life and trusted His wise timing: "If you carefully obey the commands I am giving you today, and if you love the LORD your God and serve him with all your heart and soul, then he will send the rains in their proper seasons—the early and late rains—so you can bring in your harvests of grain, new wine, and olive oil" (Deut. 11:13–14). Just as farmers patiently wait for rain in the fall and in the spring, eagerly looking for the valuable harvest to ripen, we too must be patient, taking courage, for the coming of the Lord is near (see James 5:7–8)!

DESIRE TO BE CHANGED

God's Word leaps to life for our family when Steve reads it out loud in his deep voice and dramatic presentation. The way he reads it makes us feel like we are living in the time in which it was written and experiencing it ourselves. When Steve read John 17 to me, I realized for the first time in my forty-one years of life that Jesus had prayed for me to be changed! And He had prayed for me to be changed by truth. Jesus taught us that His very words are truth and that we become more like Him by His words (see John 17:17).

I have a little Post-it note on my prayer wall that says, "Father, change me as I pray." This has become an earnest desire of my heart—to be changed. Jesus prayed that I would be made holy by His Word. What a powerful prayer by the great I AM. The answer to this prayer is a yes! What an invitation to dig deep into His Word and to know that as the Spirit teaches me the words of Jesus, *I will*, step by step, become more like my teacher. Our eager expectation comes from knowing that we will be like our Father, for we will see Him as He really is (see 1 John 3:2–3).

We are so loved as His children. Just knowing that we will be like the Father, who loves us so dearly, and that we will see Him as He really is creates in us a desire for purity here on Earth. Our purity springs forth from the Spirit dwelling within us. We desire to be holy, for He is holy (see 1 Pet. 1:16). "Satan knows well the power of true holiness, and the immense injury which increased attention to it will do to his kingdom."[1]

DESIRE FOR GOD'S GLORY

We should make it our aim to live lives that are well-pleasing to God (see 2 Cor. 5:9), which brings Him great glory. "He died for all, that those who live should live no longer for themselves, but for Him who died for them and rose again" (2 Cor. 5:15, NKJV). When we understand the gift that our Father gave us in His Son, it creates in us a huge desire for our inner and outer lives to be pleasing to Him.

We get one chance during this trip we are taking to the Celestial City, our eternal home, to point to Jesus with our lives. Andrew Murray highlights the secret to this desire to live for God's glory: "Believer, abide in Christ in times of affliction, and thou shalt bring forth more fruit. The deeper experience of Christ's tenderness and the Father's love will urge thee to live to His glory."[2]

It is our Spirit-breathed desire for our God's glory that keeps us longing to follow Him with undivided hearts. It moves us to bravely sit under His searchlight so He can uncover any places in our hearts that have been darkened by emotional wounds and walled off from His love through habits that numb our pain. Our hope for glory ahead will not disappoint. Desiring God's glory enables us to courageously ask Jesus to take off the Band-Aids we have stuck over the wounds deep within our souls, where we are bleeding from betrayal, disappointments, and regrets. When we invite Jesus to sit with our bruised hearts, His love begins to heal us from the inside out.

Our desire for His glory helps us put aside our differences with other believers and remember that we have been called out of darkness into His marvelous light (see 1 Pet. 2:9). We walk in the light as He is in the light and have fellowship with the body of Christ (see 1 John 1:7).

When Jesus promised to answer us when we pray, His one intention was that the Father would be glorified in the Son (see John 14:13). As we live fully surrendered to our captain, His Spirit within us prays, "Father, glorify Your name!"

DESIRE FOR GOD'S WILL, GOD'S WAY

Isobel Kuhn writes in her autobiography, *By Searching*, "It was not a question if I wanted to go or not—*I was no longer my own*."[3]

Isobel had accepted an invitation to a Bible and missionary conference, where she roomed with a widowed young missionary, Edna. Isobel was deeply impacted by Edna's hunger for God: "She sought the Lord's face before that of anyone else at the beginning of each day. There was no wakeup chatter and pillow-flinging nonsense at dawn. This deeply brushed heart hungered and panted after the Lord, and her first waking thought was a longing for His fellowship and presence. And she kindled the same hunger in me. Remember, I had a bruised heart, too."[4]

Isobel saw the purity of Edna's desires to follow Jesus wherever He called her, for she had been crucified with Christ, and she no longer lived, but Christ lived in her (see Gal. 2:20). It didn't matter to Isobel if she *wanted* to go overseas as a missionary; what mattered was that she knew she was no longer her own. Her desire became, "I'm Yours, God; take me where You will."

To know the cross is to know freedom. Self-denial is not a single act but a lifestyle. We take up a new life—the life of Jesus lived through His Holy Spirit within us. It is a position of our souls to desire that God's will be done. We function within our new identity as love slaves of Jesus Christ following in our teacher's footsteps.

This is not losing a thing! What we gain is *so* much more valuable! This is what Jesus taught in the parable about the kingdom of heaven being like a treasure hidden in the field, which a man found. In his joy he went and sold all that he had and bought that field (see Matt. 13:44).

CHANGING DESIRES

I have mentioned Andrew Murray several times in this book for good reason: his complete surrender and obedience led to humility and great faith. The faith he had is the same faith we have access to today, because it was in Jesus alone. Murray's desires became holy desires, shaped by his moment-by-moment, unbroken fellowship with God:

> There is deep and oft-renewed heart searching to see whether the surrender has indeed been entire; fervent prayer to the heart searching Spirit that nothing may be kept back. Everything is yielded to the power of His life in us, that it may exercise its sanctifying influence even on ordinary wishes and desires. His Holy Spirit breathes through our whole being, and without our being conscious how, our desires, as the breathings of the Divine life, are in conformity with the Divine will, and are fulfilled.[5]

It is when I have searched for unshakable peace, hope, and joy through a personal, tender attachment to Jesus Christ that I have received ongoing Whispers shaping my desires into His desires. When we wholeheartedly delight ourselves in the Lord, there is no longer a difference between our desires and His. We begin to pray powerful Spirit-authored prayers.

I am lost without His Whisper. I am left to chase my own desires and sit in my disappointments, chained to discouragement. It is His gentle voice that reminds us of what is true, especially what is true *today*. God is in the habit of influencing our desires, shaping them into the desires Jesus has for us. As we delight ourselves in Him, He gives us the desires of our hearts (see Ps. 37:4).

SURPRISED BY SUN

I opened my eyes to a new day, a new year, and a new decade. Portland, Oregon, experienced a surprise glorious sunrise on January 1, 2020. The sun rose brilliantly, coloring pinks and oranges into clouds threatening to darken our skies.

The weather forecast for New Year's Day had predicted solid rainstorms throughout the day. But the Spirit had stirred a desire in us during our family prayer time on New Year's Eve to go worship Jesus as we looked upon the vast waters of the Pacific Ocean. It is always good to hear the ocean roar louder than our trials. Despite the forecast, we crazy Engelmans decided to pack raingear and drive an hour and a half to stare into the ocean and welcome in the new year. We declared that it would be worth it, even in the rain, to be gifted a few moments of listening to the roar of the ocean, staring into its bigness, and feeling mountainous trials dwindle in size.

We rejoiced when we recognized through the shocking sunrise that God was already answering our family's New Year's Eve prayer that He would do immeasurably more than all we asked or imagined in this new year (see Eph. 3:20)! What a way to start! Beautifully displayed clouds of all shapes and sizes were placed throughout the skies overhead. As we drove toward the ocean, rainbow after rainbow made its vibrant appearance for us to enjoy.

We were reminded of God's promises and felt our hearts beat in rhythm with the joy in our souls. Our first day in 2020 with a desire for 20/20 Jesus vision was off to an amazing start!

We arrived at Cannon Beach, where God surprised us again with playtime on the beach, albeit freezing on our feet! We drew so many raised eyebrows as we ran by others dressed more sensibly. Complete strangers smiled and said, "You don't have shoes on! It's winter!" to whom we responded with gleeful sounds of Jesus joy. After we'd had our fill of fun at the beach, we took shelter in the warmth of a coffee shop to play the game Apples to Apples.

Jesus has steadfast love for us. He is always present with us. It is simply our awareness of His love and His presence that changes us. We increase this awareness through time spent in His Word with the Spirit. Sometimes it also helps to observe His handiwork in nature like our family did at the ocean on New Year's Day. That surprise sunrise that defied the predicted rainstorm was a manifestation of His love to me and my family—a reminder that although Jesus did not promise a life of ease, He promised us Himself.

Sometimes when we let go of the questions troubling us and surrender to the forecast of a winter storm, we are surprised by the brilliant sunrise of Jesus' presence flooding our souls. Peace stays whether the storm comes or goes. As we release ourselves completely into the love of our Creator, our desires become His desires through the Whisper within.

Pray It In

How good it is to be near You, God. I have made You, oh sovereign Lord, my shelter, and I will tell everyone about the wonderful things You do (see Ps. 73:28). "Teach me your ways, O Lord, that I may live according to your truth! Grant me purity of heart, so that I may honor you. With all my heart I will praise you, O Lord my God. I will give glory to your name forever, for your love for me is very great" (Ps. 86:11–13). Spirit, breathe through my entire being. Exercise Your sanctifying influence in me. Show me where my surrender has not been in full. Create in me a clean heart, and renew a right spirit within me (see Ps. 51:10). Purify me. Make me a vessel prepared for every good work (see 2 Tim. 2:21).

Jesus, thank You for taking hold of me today. I rest in Your love.

.

9

WHISPERS
PRODUCE FRUIT

My eighty-four-year-old friend Leo is the sender of my all-time favorite text message that I have saved in my journals and now share with you in this book. I am writing this exactly as my dear Leo sent it (the "WOWs" are his too!) as a Whisper to him from his Creator:

> (LOVE) Jesus said, "As the Father has loved me, so have I loved you (LEO). Now remain in my love." WOW!
>
> (JOY) Jesus said, "I am coming to you now (speaking of the Father) but I say these things while I am still in the world, so that LEO may have the full measure of my joy within HIM!" WOW!
>
> (PEACE) Jesus said, "Peace I leave with you, LEO; my peace I give to you. I do not give to you as the world gives. LEO, do not let your heart be troubled and do not be afraid." WOW-WOW-WOW.

He ended his message with, "All of the above are taught in Galatians 5:22. It is the first three of the nine gifts of the Spirit." This text from Leo turned my studies to the fruit-bearing life offered to us in Jesus Christ.

Steve and I met Leo in 2016 when we were drawn to an older gentleman reading his Bible alone at a table in the coffee corner at church. I felt the warmth of his desire to know Jesus as we walked toward him. In typical Lisa-like honesty, before even introducing myself, I blurted out with excitement, "You are the answer to my morning prayer!" Early that morning I had begged Jesus in my prayer closet to encourage us at church today through one of His people. Leo looked up at me with joy, tears gathering in his wise eyes. He pulled out chairs and asked if we might join him for a while.

We settled in beside him, learning that just a few weeks prior to this, his beautiful wife had gone home to be with Jesus. His love for Jesus shone brightly through his grief as he expressed the loneliness he felt and then described the deep companionship he was experiencing with his heavenly Father. That first meeting turned into a regular threesome gathering on Sunday mornings before our church's worship service until we parted ways to opposite sides of the country almost two years later.

Our beloved Leo is steady in his study of Scripture. We count it a deep joy to know him. His messages to me have strengthened my soul through encouragement from the Word. Leo's and my favorite passages of Scripture, which we delight in bouncing back and forth to each other, are found throughout chapters 14 to 18 of John's Gospel.

I return to John 14–18 regularly for resting in my Creator's love, for peace to envelop my entire being—*His* peace. This is not the peace our culture seeks in emptying the mind and retreating to tropical islands. This is a peace that is present despite our circumstances. Peace that comes through simplicity and obedience.

I return to these chapters in John's Gospel for joy in its fullness to abound within me. Love, joy, peace, patience, kindness, goodness, faithfulness, gentleness, and self-control are all fruits of the Spirit living within us, speaking to us and encouraging us through the written Word of God. The more time we spend in the Word, communing with the Father and Son through the Spirit, the greater our awareness will be of His life and love flowing throughout our whole *beings*.

In John 15, Jesus is described as our vine and God the Father as our attentive gardener tending to us, His branches. "A soul filled with large thoughts of the Vine will be a strong branch and will abide confidently in Him. Be much occupied with Jesus, and believe much in Him, as the true vine. I am His branch, I am in Him. I find my sufficiency in the Almighty Savior. 'I am the True Vine'— He who offers us the privilege of an actual union with Himself is the great I AM, the almighty God, who upholds all things by the Word of His power. Cultivate a trustful disposition towards God, the habit of always thinking of Him, of His ways, and His works, with bright confiding hopefulness."[1]

GOD'S WORD PRODUCES STRENGTH AND JOY

God's written Word is the primary way He speaks to us. The Holy Spirit opens our eyes to wonderful things in the Scriptures (see Ps. 119:18), teaches and reminds us of all that Jesus spoke (see John 14:26), guides us, nudges us, and communicates with us however He pleases. But it will always be in total agreement with the Scriptures.

The greater our knowledge and understanding of God's Word, the greater our comfort, the greater our joy, and the stronger we are in our vine, Jesus, from whom we receive all we need. My favorite passage of Scripture to illustrate this is found in the book of Nehemiah:

Nehemiah, who was the governor, and Ezra the priest and scribe, and the Levites who taught the people said to all the people, "This day is holy to the Lord your God; do not mourn or weep." For all the people wept as they heard the words of the Law. Then he said to them, "Go your way. Eat the fat and drink sweet wine and send portions to anyone who has nothing ready, for this day is holy to our Lord. And do not be grieved, for the joy of the Lord is your strength." So the Levites calmed all the people, saying, "Be quiet, for this day is holy; do not be grieved." And all the people went their way to eat and drink and to send portions and to make great rejoicing, because they had understood the words that were declared to them. (Neh. 8:9–12, ESV)

The people of Israel experienced a sweet calm followed by great rejoicing because after listening attentively to the Word of God, they *understood*! Regardless of any mountain looming ahead of us, the joy of the Lord is our strength. It is by faith, which comes by hearing, and hearing, which comes by the Word of God, that our weakness is turned to strength. We rejoice because we understand God's promises of *good news* that for those of us who have given our lives to Jesus Christ, the best is always yet to come!

As we spend time in God's Word, we should ask the Holy Spirit to grant us understanding. Just like the people of Israel, the more we understand, the greater our rejoicing, and the stronger we will be. Rejoicing in Christ makes us unshakable and is something we can always do.

Bearing Fruit in All Seasons

When we moved to California in the summer of 2017, we settled in a rental home just north of Temecula. I noticed that the words "joy" and "peace" were inscribed into the cement on the path lead-ing up to our front porch. This took my mind immediately to one of my favorite verses in Isaiah: "You will go out in joy and be led forth in peace; the mountains and hills will burst into song before you, and all the trees of the field will clap their hands" (Isa. 55:12, NIV). That walkway leading into our California home was my reminder that in every season of life we will bear fruit when we meditate on God's Word day and night. We will go out in joy and be led forth in peace.

> Blessed is the man who walks not in the counsel of the wicked, nor stands in the way of sinners, nor sits in the seat of scoffers; but his delight is in the law of the LORD, and on his law he meditates day and night. He is like a tree planted by streams of water that yields its fruit in its season, and its leaf does not wither. In all that he does, he prospers. (Ps. 1:1–3, ESV)

The promise in Psalm 1:1–3 is that when we meditate on God's Word day and night, we *will* bear fruit in *every* season. This includes our seasons of waiting for healing, restoration in rela-tionships, and the salvation of those we love. Through the Spirit we can lead fruit-bearing lives.

In the sixth meditation in Andrew Murray's *Waiting on God*, Murray instructs, "Let each one of us forget himself and think of the great company of God's saints throughout the world, who are waiting on Him right now."[2] Wow! This brings good news! We are not alone in our waiting. "Let us all join in this fervent prayer for each other: 'Let no one who waits on You be ashamed.' Think for a moment of the multitudes of people who need that prayer; how many there are who are sick and weary and alone, and they feel that their prayers are not being answered, who sometimes fear that their hope is in vain."[3]

Seasons of physical weakness do not sideline us from living fruit-bearing lives. "The Christian often tries to forget his weakness: God wants us to remember it, to feel it deeply. The Christian wants to conquer his weakness and to be freed from it: God wants us to rest and even rejoice in it. The Christian mourns over his weakness: Christ teaches His servant to say, 'I take pleasure in infirmities; most gladly will I glory in my infirmities.' The Christian thinks his weakness his greatest hindrance in the life and service of God: God tells us that it is the secret of strength and success. It is our weakness, heartily accepted and continually realized, that gives us our claim and access to the strength of Him who has said, 'My *strength* is made perfect in *weakness.*'"[4] In seasons of waiting and seasons of afflictions, Christ will manifest Himself strong in us, producing the Spirit's fruit.

WHOLEHEARTED CHRIST FOLLOWERS

Has Jesus won our hearts? *All* of our hearts? Is there a little corner in our hearts set up for self-occupancy? Has His love flooded every crevice? Are we fully surrendered?

One Sunday our local pastor spoke about parenting by winning our children's hearts rather than demanding their obedience. When we do, our children will tend to obey us gladly. In the same way, he taught us, when our Lord has won our hearts, we too will wholeheartedly follow Him. We will not live stuck in discouragement or defeated by fear. We will not be spiritually weakened because of fostering bad attitudes. We will recognize that discontentment is contagious, but contentment is too.

We become like Jesus when we spend time with Him. In the same way that we receive by faith our salvation, we will receive by faith our sanctification—our growing in likeness to Jesus as we live in constant conversation with Him. The private practice of spending time with Jesus in our early morning quiet times will bring about in us the capacity to hear His voice. We will quickly recognize His gentle redirections throughout our days, leading to fruit-bearing lives. The Lord will show us ever so gently when bad habits are starting to take root in us, enabling us to return once again to intense closeness with Him.

As I listened to my pastor's sermon, I thought of the sweet truth that it is God's kindness that leads us to repentance (see Titus 3:4). How much more may our kindness, which is Jesus in us, be what leads others to repentance that results in their turning and going the way of Jesus. "Kindness has converted more sinners than zeal, eloquence, or learning."[5]

Becoming a wholehearted, singularly focused Christ follower results in a fruitful life marked by joyful obedience. This obedience is not a burden; it is a beautiful love response from our acute awareness of Jesus' love for us. "This is the love of God, that we keep his commandments. And his commandments are not burdensome" (1 John 5:3, ESV). One of the fruits of our obedience is our happiness! "Happy are those who keep His testimonies, who seek Him with a whole heart" (Ps. 119:2, TLV).

WATCHING FOR THORNS

In the parable of the sower, found in Luke 8:4–15, Jesus teaches us to watch out for conditions of our hearts that prevent us from living fruit-bearing lives. We need to guard our hearts, for they are the wellspring of life (see Prov. 4:23). Jesus teaches that His Word can be choked out by thorns, which are the cares of this world: pleasures and riches. These do not truly satisfy. *Nothing* satisfies like our Jesus!

To be fruit-filled, prospering Christians, we must drink deeply from the living water and graze continuously on the green pastures of His Word, which is our *life*! Jesus tends to any soil in us that begins to turn rocky by our return to old habits of the past, which harden our hearts against the work He desires to do in and through us. It is a daily habit, not a one-and-done experience, to come to Jesus. We come to Him to *stay* with Him. "Sin has disturbed all relations. . . . Peace can only come with right. Where everything is as God would have it, in God's order and in harmony with His will, there alone can peace reign. Jesus Christ came to restore peace on earth, and peace in the soul, by restoring righteousness."[6] "My flesh continues to rise and lead me to evil. But my Father is the Husbandman, He grafted me into the life of His Son and the Holy Life of Jesus is mightier than my evil life."[7]

Psalm 119 is filled with connections on God's Word to light and life—our protection from the thorny cares of the world. Below are just two small bites of the delicious soul food found there:

> Remember the word to Your servant, upon which You have caused me to hope. This is my comfort in my affliction, for Your word has given me life. (Ps. 119:49–50, NKJV)
>
> Forever, O LORD, Your word is settled in heaven. Your faithfulness endures to all generations; You established the earth, and it abides. They continue this day according to Your ordinances, for all are Your servants. Unless Your law had been my delight, I would then have perished in my affliction. I will never forget Your precepts, for by them You have given me life. (Ps. 119:89–93, NKJV)

In *Praying the Scriptures for Your Children,* Jodie Berndt crafted a prayer from the parable of the sower. I have used it consistently over my family in my morning prayer times in my effort to watch for thorns in our lives:

> Let _____ 's heart be good soil, that he might hear your word, retain it, and persevere to produce a crop of godly

character and effectiveness for your kingdom. Don't let Satan snatch your word from _____ 's heart, and don't let the worries, riches, or pleasures of this life choke your word and make it unfruitful in his life. Let his roots go down deep, so he can stand firm in times of testing (Luke 8:11–15).[8]

Vine-Ripened Blackberries

Here in the Pacific Northwest blackberries abound. In my backyard they creep over the fence during most of August. Our children take our step stool to harvest their blackberry snack each afternoon. They have learned that the yummiest berries are deep purple, bursting with flavor in their mouths. Sometimes they get impatient and pick the ones that are still partly red, learning the hard way as their mouths pucker in distaste.

Like He does with blackberries, our Father is doing ripening work in each of us. He, the gardener, through His Spirit, keeps us in His vine, the beloved Son. We remain there, trusting in His perfect eye to see when the fruit He is producing through us is ready for harvest, full of flavor, and bursting with His goodness.

When we remain in the vine under His watchful eye, we receive His love through every season of life, rain or shine. In the Pacific Northwest, it's the spring rains and summer sun that deepen the green and produce a bounty from the land. Not only do we spend seasons of waiting on the Father for the desires of our heart and fulfillment of our prayers, but He, as a Father filled with love for His child, waits on us, closely tending to the fruit ripening on the vine. "Therefore will the Lord wait, that he may be gracious unto you, and therefore will he be exalted, that he may have mercy upon you: for the Lord is a God of judgment: blessed are all they that wait for him" (Isa. 30:18, KJV).

FRUIT FROM REST

I heard the familiar sound of little feet about to sneak into my prayer closet (shh, don't tell Steve!). This time, rather than the usual Sammy J face rounding the corner, it was my Gracie girl, now eight years old. She said, "Momma! I'm starting a prayer wall too! Let's ask Jesus to help Sammy J not to be afraid of cats anymore! Can you help me put one up, Momma?"

I smiled big, whispering my praise to Jesus in recognition of *His* fruit produced by the Spirit nudging me to choose rest: To stop. Surrender. Remain. Be still. Simply *be*. He used my imperfect example to stir the hearts of *both* my girls to put up their own prayer walls, to read their Bibles in the mornings, and to ask questions.

It's not our natural tendency to slow our schedules and still our souls, yet it is the necessary means by which fruit ripens in our lives. "Remain in *me*, and I will remain in you" (John 15:4). When we remain in Jesus, it results in a "full of fruit" life. Our *being* will result in our *doing*. Apart from Jesus, we can do nothing (see John 15:5). We will be surprised by the joy of self-forgetfulness when we take time to be still before the Lord. We will be more productive in the tasks God has beckoned us to and less busy about the things that aren't for us in our seasons of life.

To produce lasting fruit, we must do this one thing: *remain*, or stay in the place we have been occupying.[9] We must open up our hands that are clinging to whatever it is that we hold dear and release it all to the One who is Himself our most precious possession. We must remain listening and still. This is how we bear His fruit—staying in that safe place with our Father, who knows all that we need and is delighted by our nearness. It's like Sammy, who is seven years old now yet is still the happiest when he is snuggled next to me. It is a delight to my heart.

THE PROSPERITY OF GOD'S WORD

The written voice of God powerfully produces fruit, prospering everywhere God sends it. Isaiah declares,

> It is the same with my word. I send it out, and it always produces fruit. It will accomplish all I want it to, and it will prosper everywhere I send it. (Isa. 55:11)

Truths from Isaiah 55:11:

- *God* sends His Word out.
- It *always* produces fruit.
- It *will* accomplish His desires.
- It *will* prosper everywhere He sends it.

All creation came about through the Word of God and the Spirit of God: "By the word of the LORD the heavens were made, and by the breath of his mouth all their host" (Ps. 33:6, ESV). Every time God speaks a word, it is carried by His breath, the Spirit. Through His Word and through His Spirit, God makes His home with us as we love and obey His Word.

The Word, Jesus, became flesh and dwelt among us (see John 1:14). God then showed His great love for us in that while we were yet sinners, Jesus died for us (see Rom. 5:8). Jesus died and rose again the third day in accordance with the Scriptures (see 1 Cor. 15:3–4). This became the gospel, the *good news* that goes out to prosper wherever it is sent.

Paul spoke of the fruit-bearing life produced by the Word in his letter to the church in Colossae:

> We always pray for you, and we give thanks to God, the Father of our Lord Jesus Christ. For we have heard of your

faith in Christ Jesus and your love for all of God's people, which come from your confident hope of what God has reserved for you in heaven. You have had this expectation ever since you first heard the truth of the Good News.

This same Good News that came to you is going out all over the world. It is bearing fruit everywhere by changing lives, just as it changed your lives from the day you first heard and understood the truth about God's wonderful grace. (Col. 1:3–6)

The good news that comes from Christ will change us and produce fruit-bearing lives. But John 10:10 is a caution for us: the enemy comes to steal, kill, and destroy; Jesus, however, came for us to bear fruit and live life to the fullest. The truly abundant life is one filled with the fruits of the Spirit. The world cannot produce this true prosperity and cannot stop it. God's Word will triumph.

The Power of Moments

Life is filled with choices as to how we will spend time, energy, and love. The little moments of life add up to big change by the end of a lifetime when we seek to spend them well: a few minutes here and there to sit with our child and listen to his or her musings; a prayer for a friend while stopped at a red light; a smile and a conversation to the people behind us in a long line at the grocery store. Maybe we get up a few minutes earlier to slow down our mornings just a bit. Maybe we choose to spend a few moments watching the clouds move ever so slowly across the big sky. The Spirit in us is powerful beyond comprehension to lead us in paths of righteousness for His name's sake (see Ps. 23:3).

When Jesus moved our family back to our beloved Portland area in late spring of 2019, He plopped us down right by a nature park filled with miles of hiking trails. He provided a rental home with green space behind us, towering trees of all kinds, and the daily visits of wildlife friends outside my bedroom window. I love to observe our backyard for a few minutes after waking up each day. Sometimes a little blue jay is peeking at me from the tree branch, or a squirrel is engaged in a game of early morning tag. When I slow myself for a moment, I can hear my Creator's love in the footsteps of my husband moving through his morning routine, which sometimes includes making us fresh juice to start the day. I receive precious morning squeeze hugs from each of my four not-so-little children.

Not only did Jesus plop us down right by a nature park, but He also moved us to within a ten-minute drive from our close friends whom we had missed so dearly during our two years in California. We find power in the moments we choose to gather with others, giving and receiving the love of our Creator within the framework of friendship, which He designed. We must fight for time to foster our friendships. I never regret the times I slip out to meet this precious heart whom I live by. I love the moments we sneak in just to be together. Sometimes I cry. Sometimes she does. More often than not, we both laugh, and we both cry. The tears we share together with our Father who is always with us are holy tears. Having her just ten minutes away is a joy to my soul. When I am with her, I feel the love of Jesus in her presence. Her "with me" heart in my difficulties is a gift into eternity that I know we will celebrate from the safety of heaven's shores.

Our dearest friends will never be perfect, and at times they may disappoint us, just as we are not perfect and may disappoint them. Our friends are gifts from God to show us more of Himself and to be His tangible love to us. I am grateful for my comrades of the cross—friends who long to live and love like Jesus. We receive strength of soul in the moments we choose to gather with friends. The hours here and there add up to great change over a lifetime of friendship.

THE FRUIT OF FREEDOM

Through the cross, Jesus whispers to us about freedom. When Jesus stretched His hands out on that cross, it was love that ran red as payment for our sins. Because of His perfect sinless life, death, and victorious resurrection, we can live in freedom.

Those arms He opened on the cross remain open to receive us despite our wrong choices. Those Savior arms are an invitation for us to come just as we are. Jesus awaits us with a listening ear, restoration, peace, hope, joy, and the truly abundant Spirit-filled, fruit-producing life. Stepping into His arms is stepping into freedom. Jesus whispers to us that whoever He sets free is free indeed (see John 8:36)—free from eternal separation from God; free from shame, guilt, regrets, bitterness; free to forgive others as we have been forgiven. We joyfully serve one another in love because of our freedom (see Gal. 5:1).

When we run into our Creator's arms, His love enters our entire beings and changes the course of our earthly lives. One day we will look deep into His eyes. Oh, I just want to stop and imagine it right now! The color. The tenderness. The twinkle. The impossibly big love. Even now God has fixed the eye of His sovereign love upon us![10] When we fasten our eyes on that love, we know we do not lack a thing. We lie down in green pastures in obedience. We have joy, peace, and every fruit produced by the Spirit.

When we choose to go our own ways, we lose the sound of our Father's heartbeat in the world's noise. He becomes dangerously small in our minds' eyes. We start to doubt the power of His grace to change the circumstances of our life—or to uphold us *through* them. We lose our freedom; we don't gain it.

Chains of love keep us close to our Beloved, protecting us from letting unrest, doubts, despair, and discouragement become our normal. This love encourages our complete trust in the boundaries of our circumstances. He is in control of them! I see in my mind a safe pasture with a fence around it. His Spirit decides the size of the pasture. The fence is the circumstances of our lives.

We can experience the heights and depths of humility through tender communion with Jesus. Remembering that we are nothing takes us to the depths, yet when we remember that Christ in us is everything, we can be carried to the heights, undefeated because Jesus is our victory! We are on the winning side! When we choose surrender and live in obedience and trust, we can experience the Spirit's fruit of joy, peace, and rest in our Creator's love.

Pray It In

I listen carefully to You, Father. You speak peace to Your faithful people (see Ps. 85:8). Let my heart be good soil, that I would persevere and bear fruit for Your kingdom (see Luke 8:15). My delight is in Your Word, Lord, and I meditate on it day and night. I will be like a tree planted by streams of water, bearing fruit in season, whose leaves will not wither. In all I do, I will prosper (see Ps. 1:2–3). Thank You, Father, that You love me. Let Your love in me overflow to others (see 1 John 4:7, 11, 18).

Jesus, thank You for taking hold of me today. I rest in Your love.

10

WHISPERS
LIGHTEN LOADS

Last week I enjoyed a half-hour drive to the small town where my friend lives. Upon entering her door for a visit, the sight of her welcoming smile brought emotions I hadn't known I was feeling! I held myself together for several minutes while my kids took off their shoes and ran off to play before bursting into tears. The words that tumbled out of my mouth as she hugged me surprised me: "I miss time with my good friends!"

We live in a world in which loneliness is spreading like a dormant virus. It begins as a silent intruder without symptoms. That's how it started for me this last summer in 2019. I had returned to the Portland area after almost two years in California. We were so excited to be returning that we hadn't given much thought to how different it might be from when we had lived there before. Not only had our previous community expanded into what had been nearby countryside, but our children were now older and bigger! Playdates were changing as our children's interests and abilities changed.

My energy for engaging in friendships also seemed to be shrinking as my children grew. This too came as a surprise! I had mistakenly thought that the older my children became, the *more* time and energy I would have for investing in friendships. But the one-room playdates of toddlerhood turned into exploring big parks. Little ears became big ears. This created a need to meet with my friends alone for conversations that turned toward what filled the painful rooms in our souls. My days grew full with navigating new phases of parenting and connecting with the blossoming hearts of my children. *How could I reach outside my home to add anything else to a plate filled to overflowing with the happenings within my own four walls?*

My dear friend's hug brought to my awareness the virus of loneliness that had made its home within me. Loneliness is the cry of our souls for the friendships we were divinely designed for. Jesus sometimes brings His Whisper of love through the arms of our comrades.

Friendship is worth our effort. Friendship is worth asking Jesus to help us make space for on our overflowing plates. Our friends gift us listening ears, words of wisdom, different perspectives to consider, shared sorrows and joys. Sometimes we've cried out every drop of strong faith that we have, and our friends step close and hold us up in the way Aaron and Hur held up Moses' arms. They intercede for us when our capacity to voice a prayer is absent.

When I find myself crying out for friendship, I first remember that Jesus is my faithful friend, my ever-present companion, comforter, and counselor. He modeled friendship within the triune Godhead, with His heavenly Father and the Holy Spirit, creating us in His image with a need for friendship. With Jesus by my side, I remember that friendship was His idea.

As I spent time with my dear friend that day, I received an encouraging Whisper from the Lord for my soul through her hugs and our conversation. Her words of wisdom pointed me to God's purposeful design of Lisa Engelman. I left with a renewed bounce in my step, a warmed heart, and a new acceptance of the introvert that I am.

At times the best gift we can give to a friend is being okay with him or her not being okay. Surprisingly, our friend will often leave our presence just a few steps closer to being okay because of the love of Jesus that travels through our arms in a big squeeze hug as His Whisper that bears our friend's burden. Jesus has a way of lightening the loads of His followers through His gentle voice within us, His Word, and His body (our fellow believers). In this chapter I will share several ways this has happened for me. But as each of us grows in our own awareness of God's voice within us, we should be ready to experience it in our own unique ways.

DIVINE DESIGN

When my children's homeschooling time is complete and afternoon arrives, I am ready to melt into the rocking chair that faces my bedroom window. Outside are towering evergreen trees with massive maple trees alongside. When the wind kicks up, my soul gets lost in its song as I watch the branches sway. I am learning that my introverted self has this need for recharging alone—it is what helps me remain able to minister to others. Most days I exit the quiet hour with a renewed mind and increased energy.

As I turned the corner into my forties a couple years ago, Jesus began moving my soul closer to peaceful acceptance of the "me" that He put together. Jesus purposed for me to fulfill good works in Him that, by divine design and equipping, can only be completed through my life.

By my Creator's design, I am an introvert who is at times extroverted on purpose. I love people. But I grow tired after gathering with others. I love my children. But after a few hours of loud activity, the "system fail" light on my nervous system begins to flash.

When I choose to listen to the Whisper within nudging me to take some quiet time with Him, He lightens whatever load I have strapped onto my shoulders. He leads me in my yes and no answers as He manages my time in accordance with my energy allotment for the day.

In those quiet recharge hours, He speaks to me about who I am in Him, reminding me to steer clear of wondering how other disciples of Jesus Christ seem to handle so much more than I can. In making decisions for our yeses and no's, our best compass is Jesus and His Word, not the lives of other people. What is right for others is not necessarily what is right for us. In our decision making we must await His Whisper assuring us, *"This is the way for you; walk in it"* (see Isa. 30:21).

By divine design, my introverted self needs to space out gatherings a bit, to schedule in recovery days, to say no to some good activities, and sometimes to giggle with joy when I am left alone in my house for a few hours of silence. These rhythms have allowed for joyful obedience to write or attend to other assignments for my numbered days as God's ambassador. It is also by God's design that I have experienced a sudden filling of the Spirit for divine appointments and ministry that I would never have imagined that I was equipped for. This is our God. He can do anything He wants, however He wants, whenever He wants. He seems to specialize in choosing weak vessels, for in doing so He alone gets the glory!

DROPPING OUR BACKPACKS

One of the favorite books I have enjoyed reading with all four of my children is *Little Pilgrim's Progress* by Helen Taylor, a children's version of John Bunyan's *Pilgrim's Progress*. Little Christian travels from his home in the City of Destruction toward the Celestial City under the burden of his backpack until he arrives at the cross. When we came to this part in the story, to show the children how weighty sin and sorrow can be, one by one I stuffed heavy books into the backpacks they wore on their backs. Laughter erupted as Sammy J fell over backward before he could even take a step! Little Christian's journey was easier after he dropped his burdens at the cross.

The life of a Christ follower is marked by lightness. Jesus died and rose again to create a way for us to live in right standing with God and be freed from the weight of our sin. The victorious Christian life is marked by faith that defeats sin. This happens when we trust Jesus to deliver us from *sin* today, the same way we trusted that He paid for our sins on the cross. For some reason, faith for salvation has a childlike simplicity to it. Indeed we *do* believe that Jesus paid for our sins; He alone could do it! But do we also believe, in *this* moment, that His power delivers us from being in bondage to sin, choice by choice?

One morning during our Bible time, the children and I were making our way through 1 John 3 and came to this verse: "No one born of God makes a practice of sinning, for God's seed abides in him; and he cannot keep on sinning, because he has been born of God" (1 John 3:9, ESV). Ellie asked, "*Why* do we still sin?" *Oh, dear daughter!* I thought. *How many times have I asked myself the same thing about my own sin!*

I told her that we are all on a journey, just like little Christian in our story. When we choose to stay close to Jesus, He has control over us, and He helps us not to sin. He is also right there to forgive us and to take that brick out of our backpack when we do mess up. But when we step away from Him and go our own ways, our backpacks fill up with bricks of sin, regret, guilt, shame, fears, failures, doubts, disappointments, and our own expectations of ourselves.

Jesus implores us, "Come." Just as Christian experienced the Whisper of forgiveness when he dropped his burden, we too can walk forgiven and free when we drop our backpacks at the foot of His cross.

I Am Not Everyone's Answer

As a kid in Sunday school, when in doubt as to the correct answer to a question, yelling out "Jesus!" was usually a safe answer. How much more is Jesus the answer for the many needs around us today! Yet it has taken me until the past couple years to realize that "Lisa" is not necessarily the immediate answer to everyone's needs. To discern my yes and my no, I must stay in continual conversation with Jesus and listen for His response before I give mine.

My limitations plead with me to lighten my calendar when I feel overwhelmed. One morning in my closet, my eyes scanned my prayer wall, looking for encouragement. I read a Post-it note I had written during a season when many hearts around me were in desperate need of hope and help. It read, "I am united with the Great I AM who upholds all things by the Word of His power" (see Col. 1:17). As I read it again and again, the familiar Whisper rose up: *Lisa, you are not the answer for everyone's heartaches and trials. Yes, pray. And pray expecting Me to bring others the sustaining grace and help that I promise. But I will not always use you as the vessel through which I answer.*

The Lord can and *will* help those I love through His own creative means when I am not His chosen answer. The Lord exchanges our heavy burdens for His light yoke when we prayerfully prioritize the many pressing needs that surround us by trusting and obeying His voice.

Personality factors into how hard this can be, especially for those of us who want to fix the pain behind every tear that falls! We want to *do* something! It has taken me being debilitated through ongoing health struggles, including my cancer journey, to get me to sit down at the Lord's feet and experience the power of prayer—to remember that prayer *is* doing something. Something *big*. Talking with Jesus settles my soul. I cannot do it all. I cannot even do most of it. I am clearly not supermom or superwoman, but I serve a mighty God who fills me with His supernatural Spirit!

Some days I still feel like I am letting everyone down. Saying no is painfully difficult for me. But Jesus has helped me slow down and ask Him before saying yes with my emotions that long so much for the happiness of others. The secret to victory over the soul struggles of people pleasing is spending much time in the Word with the Spirit. The voice of truth quiets the lies that are directing our behavior and moves us in the direction of trusting His Word over our feelings.

God's voice of truth reminds us that we are loved by our Father without condition, which means that His love for us is not dependent on how well we are taking care of everyone in our lives. Remembering how much He naturally loves us increases the outward flow of His love through us toward others. As He fills us up, He sends us out as vessels of His love. The key is to spend much time with Jesus so that we act on truth rather than feelings. I love what Fénelon teaches: "If you are absorbed in God, you will be less eager to please men, but you will please them more."[1]

When life resembles an avalanche threatening to break loose, we can practice the power of the pause, retreating into the inner chambers of our hearts to listen for that gentle Whisper within. "Lord?" we whisper. We wait. He responds. He is present. He can and will help us, guiding us to His yes and His no. We remember His sufficiency for our current concerns. He floods us with a fresh wave of love, reminding us who we are in Him and who He is in us.

Jesus *is* the answer to the cry of hearts all around. As we persevere in prayer, sometimes He will use us to be His tangible love—or He may send another.

BITTERNESS CRUSHES LIFE

The load of bitterness is heavy. It is poison to our souls. Bitterness sidelines us from the race we are called to run and brings us trouble: "Work at living in peace with everyone, and work at living a holy life, for those who are not holy will not see the Lord. Look after each other so that none of you fails to receive the grace of God. Watch out that no poisonous root of bitterness grows up to trouble you, corrupting many" (Heb. 12:14–15). Bitterness diminishes our laughter, joy, hope, and fulfillment in Jesus Christ that He gives us when we obey His command to "keep on loving each other as brothers and sisters" (Heb. 13:1).

Sometimes the pain caused by conflict stays. Perhaps we have done what we can to be at peace with others, but pain is still present despite our attempts. Rather than allowing bitterness to take root, we can turn to our comforter within us to remind us of the love God has for us. "The Holy Spirit is the Comforter, not only because He can suggest comforting thoughts of God's love but far more, because He makes us holy, and brings us into close union with Christ and with God. He teaches us to abide in Christ; and because God is found there, the truest comfort will come there too. In Christ, the heart of the Father is revealed, and higher comfort there cannot be than to rest in the Father's bosom."[2]

CASTING OUTCOMES ONTO THE FATHER

When I was diagnosed with cancer two days before Christmas in 2013, I was handed a list of possible outcomes from the doctor's clipboard. With an apologetic voice, he told me the percentages of my chances of being alive in both five years and ten years, with shrinking percentages apparently not worth mentioning after that. A Whisper came that freed me from the weight of statistics: *"Only I can tell you the future before it even happens. Everything I plan will come to pass, for I do whatever I wish"* (see Isa. 46:10).

God will work everything out according to His plan (see Eph. 1:11)! My peace over the years has come from remembering God's authority over my entire being. If I am strong, I remember that by strength no man will prevail (see 1 Sam. 2:9). If I am weak, I know that my life is upheld by God (see Ps. 54:4). "The best-equipped army cannot save a king, nor is great strength enough to save a warrior. Don't count on your warhorse to give you victory—for all its strength, it cannot save you" (Ps. 33:16–17).

When was the last time your body was at ease for an hour, or a day, or how about a week? I mean *completely* at ease. No tightness in those shoulders, no ache camping out in the heart, no concerns of upcoming tasks or events. Truly at rest.

This question troubled me during my recent trip through Dallas Willard's *Renovation of the Heart.* Repentant tears poured down my face as I realized that I could not remember a pattern of deep rest throughout my body since my entrance into motherhood more than twelve years ago. I cried out my longing to God to teach me His rest. Between parenting, cancer, and years of navigating chronic health issues, my whole being—body, heart, mind, and soul—needed renovation. I wanted to be at ease whether "dis-ease" was present or not.

Willard's book helped me understand that all of life is lived from the heart. As our hearts undergo renovation, our minds and bodies are affected. This is part of the abundant blessing of being under the Spirit's rule. One of the changes to our hearts that affect our bodies has to do with making time for Sabbath rest: "Rest is one primary mark of the condition of Sabbath in the body, as unrest is a mark of its absence."[3]

Another heart change that brought me rest was realizing that while we should properly nourish, exercise, and rest our bodies because they are holy—owned and inhabited by God— we should not idolize them, because God has control over and responsibility for them.[4] What a relief!

Willard's book challenged me to release my body to the Lord—to take time to come before the Lord and present my body to Him as a living sacrifice (see Rom. 12:1), verbally naming any areas of concern and asking Him to take charge of my body, fill it with His life, and use it for His purposes. For example, I have come before Him and asked Him to take charge of my immune system, which has been in a weakened state ever since chemo: "Lord, I release my immune system to You. Take charge of it. Fill it with Your life, and use it for Your purposes."[5]

Feeling the peace that enveloped me after releasing years of holding onto responsibility and outcomes for my health encouraged me to begin to release the people in my life to my Father: "Lord, I release Luke to you, my precious firstborn son. Take charge of him. Fill him with Your life, and use Him for Your purposes!" I repeated this for each of my children. I now practice this on a regular basis when I sense that I have picked back up the burden of outcomes in my life. Willard teaches that Sabbath is a condition in which "we come to a place where we can joyously 'do no work'" because "God is so exalted in our minds and bodies that we can trust him with our life and our world and can take our hands off of them."[6]

We can either seize control of or release what troubles us to our Father on a daily basis. When we choose to cast our concerns on Him, remembering His tender care for us (see 1 Pet. 5:7), we will experience the liberty of untroubled souls. It will show up as a spring in our steps and smiles on our faces.

"A horse is prepared for the day of battle, but victory comes from ADONAI" (Prov. 21:31, TLV). I give my best efforts to a healthy lifestyle, but I cast the outcome of my days onto my Father, who decided the number of them before time began (see Ps. 139:16). Just as children persist in asking parents for good gifts, so we should pray fervently for His intervention. Like a weaned child with its mother, we can calm and quiet our souls, resting in our perfect Father's love as our highest good (see Ps. 131:2).

Restful Work

Sometimes the good we set out to do becomes a suffocating burden. We started out in faith, obeying God. But somewhere along the way, we lost sight of Jesus as self-effort crept in. Discouragement and exhaustion followed. Perhaps in our work, we strayed from the command, "Work willingly at whatever you do, as though you were working for the Lord rather than for people" (Col. 3:23), to working for that next dopamine hit of human praise. But God's love flooding our hearts through His Spirit within us will free us from living in bondage to human approval.

Our heavenly Father's praise is sweet to the soul and so *everlasting*! The secret to restful work is found in Ephesians 6:10: "Be strong in the Lord and in His mighty power." Strength in self will result in burnout. Strength in Jesus flows powerfully throughout our whole beings when we make His heart our home—our safe haven.

The apostle Paul teaches us that this strength that comes from Jesus doesn't necessarily mean that we are delivered from our weaknesses but that we are strong *in* our weaknesses (see 2 Cor. 12:9). That's *good news*! That means that even if we are plagued by persistent weaknesses in this life, we can absolutely be *strong* in the Lord. "When the union with Christ is rejoiced in as our highest good, and everything sacrificed for the sake of maintaining it, the power will work: 'His strength will be made perfect in our weakness.'"[7]

Whispers from the Garden

One evening while Steve was away on a business trip, I sat on our couch with the children to read from *The Jesus Storybook Bible* by Sally Lloyd-Jones. Jesus was facing His darkest hour in the garden of Gethsemane, while His three closest friends slept. His arrest and crucifixion lay heavy on His Savior soul. I stopped at the sentence "Jesus walked ahead . . . alone . . . into the dark night.

He needed to talk to His heavenly Father."[8] Ever been there? Facing something so dark and crushing that in your inner being you whisper along with Jesus, "Father?"

Suddenly I longed to be alone with my heavenly Father. I stuffed my emotions just long enough to finish the story and tuck the children into their beds. Then I went to the quiet of my room, lay down on my bedroom floor, and told my heavenly Father all about it. My aches came first. Then my questions, expressing every insufficiency tumbling around my mind.

His presence lightened my load, reminding me that His understanding is greater than any situation I face (see Ps. 147:5). That's the Whisper from the garden of Gethsemane today: "*We are never, ever alone.*" When Jesus asked if there was any other way than the path before Him, an angel was sent to minister to Him (see Luke 22:42–43). Sometimes we are delivered *through* the trial, not from it. God's Word is the stable light shining into every dark hour. From the garden we learn from Jesus the path to eternal joy: "Your will, Father, Your way."

Greater Than Our Feelings— Without a Single Fault

Guilt crushes the soul. I was reading through 1 John and came across 3:20: "Even if we feel guilty, God is greater than our feelings, and he knows everything." Wow! God is greater than our feelings? How often have we struggled with feeling guilty when we have messed up yet again? God's Word is His spoken promise to us. Through 1 John 3:20, He whispers to us that we are declared not guilty, and our feelings cannot alter that truth. Jesus died to set us free from guilt; it is *only* because of His blood that we do not bear guilt.

"All glory to God, who is able to keep you from falling away and will bring you with great joy into his glorious presence without a single fault. All glory to him who alone is God, our Savior through Jesus Christ our Lord. All glory, majesty, power, and authority are his before all time, and in the present, and beyond all time! Amen" (Jude 1:24–25).

God will one day bring us with great joy into His glorious presence *without a single fault*! How can this be? I will stand before God without a single fault? My Father will be bringing me *joyously* into His presence? Thank You, Lord!

WHISPERS HEAL

The door squeaked open. I heard the familiar rhythm of Sammy J's feet traveling the worn path to my side of the bed. He climbed in for some morning snuggles and asked if I was feeling any better yet. After two weeks of an intense cold, I was more than ready to be done with it!

My cough answered his question before I could.

"Momma, I want Jesus to touch you with His hands and heal you. Let's pray!" He proceeded to pray with childlike simplicity that Jesus would make me better. My soul sang praise to Jesus as I was encouraged by his faith. Sammy knows who makes us better!

"I am the LORD who heals you" (Exod. 15:26). Jesus is our Healer, not just for colds and cancer, but for silent wounds embedded deep within our souls. When we have a broken leg, people approach us and express their concern. The broken places within that bleed painfully, however, remain hidden from those around us. These invisible wounds weigh down our hearts.

When we bravely open the doors to our deepest inner beings, His healing words penetrate deep into our hearts. They bring life to us when we find them and healing to our whole bodies (see Prov. 4:20–22). He heals the brokenhearted and bandages our wounds (see Ps. 147:3). Jesus died and rose again to give us His life so that we could be healed and whole in our oneness with Him. We can ask God to help us see ourselves not as broken but as beautifully held together in Jesus Christ, healed and whole in our union with Him (see Col. 1:17)!

LOVE LIGHTENS LOADS

Our heavenly Father loves us and keeps us safe in the care of Jesus Christ (see Jude 1:1). This love from our heavenly Father is the love that the Father has for His only begotten Son, Jesus, who continues to reveal the heart of our Father to us (see John 17:26)! How can it be? We are loved by our Father with the same love He has for His only begotten Son! This love is *in* us; Jesus is *in* us. Jesus is revealing our Father to us. The love of our Creator King is so deep, so wonderfully mysterious. I keep unwrapping it and never get to the end of my unwrapping.

Scripture soothes, restores, strengthens, and builds up what life's circumstances have flattened. When circumstances seem too big, Jesus in His patient love frequently reminds me to "just do today." How often I find tomorrow's potential burdens weighing down my shoulders. Jesus teaches us in Matthew 6 that He longs for us not to lug around tomorrow's troubles (see Matt. 6:34). It is His heart of love for us that moves Him to teach us. When we choose to obey, we receive fresh waves of His love through His Spirit.

Love has always been, it is with us today, and it always will be—for God is *love* (see 1 John 4:8). God is outside of time. Because of His love, what we call terminal becomes temporary. Sighing will end. Sorrow will flee. Grief will be no more. Jesus came and made His home with us (see John 1:14). He will return to wipe away every tear and put a final end to death, making His home once again and forevermore with His people (see Rev. 21:1–4).

When we are grounded in God's promises, our trials bring pain but not surprise. We take heart because our King overcomes!

CARRIED BY OUR FATHER

It happened again. There I sat in my seat at our church in Southern California with tears running hard down my cheeks. Among the rows of little feet packing the aisles of the church and the stage stood my three youngest children singing "Christmas Time" by Phil Wickham. The scene rewound the film of my life back to the Christmas season when cancer had been discovered in my body. Sammy J, still just a baby, was too young to be onstage at the time. But my little daughters, Gracie and Ellie, with the other children in their class were singing Christmas songs on the church stage of our local Bible study group. I remember clearly the fear racing through me that day, hijacking my joy. I was lost in the turmoil of wondering how many more Christmases I would be on Earth to cheer my children on.

Now I've had six years of watching them, teaching them, and being present with them. Ellie, who used to cry and need me to sit with her onstage, was the *most* excited of the three, pleading to go early! She even wanted French braids and said she wanted to look beautiful in her Christmas dress. Praise be to God! Oh, how these children have grown! It is the earnest prayer of my heart that they would continue to grow in wisdom and stature, in favor with man and God (see Luke 2:52).

The Whisper that rose from God's Word as I cried my way through their Christmas performance was, "*I am the Lord who carries you*" (see Isa. 46:4). I am now in my seventh year since my cancer diagnosis. Jesus has upheld me, provided for me in miraculous ways, sustained my life, and led me along paths of righteousness for His name's sake (see Ps. 23:3). I have story after story of God's provision and faithfulness that rise in praise to the One who has upheld my life. Singing God's praise brings a lightness of heart.

When life grows heavy, we should return to the cross. Kneeling down, we can ease our burden-filled backpacks off our tired souls.

Jesus can then take out the bricks one by one, gently reminding us to cast our cares on Him because He cares for us (see 1 Pet. 5:7). As His Whispers lighten our loads, our souls can rest, calmed and quieted by the steady flow of His love within.

Pray It In

Lord, You created me and ransomed me. You have called me by name, and I am Yours. When I go through deep waters, You will be with me. When I go through rivers of difficulty, I will not drown. When I walk through the fire of oppression, I will not be burned up; the flames will not consume me (see Isa. 43:1–3). I bring my trials to You. The odds are never against me, Father, because You are for me (see Rom. 8:31). Thank You for loving me! Thank You for keeping me safe in the care of Your Son, Jesus (see Jude 1:1). I come to You, God, my only safe haven (see Ps. 43:2). You lift up those who are weighed down (see Ps. 146:8). Lord, shepherd me and carry me forever (see Ps. 28:9).

Jesus, thank You for taking hold of me today. I rest in Your love.

11

WHISPERS
DIRECT STEPS

Peace wrapped around me as I gazed at the endless green out the jet's tiny window. It was my first trip to Oregon, but before the wheels of the plane touched down in Portland, I felt like I was coming home. The peace filling me was evidence of the voice of the Holy Spirit assuring me that I was stepping obediently along His chosen path for me.

This trip took place a few months after that night in my junior year of high school when I hadn't been able to sleep because of the letter I had received from a college in Oregon and thrown in the trash (see chapter 5). I'd had a distinct sensation that I would be awake all night if I didn't get up and rescue that letter from its trip to the city dump. I had decided that I would open it, read it, and toss it right back in the trash can. But God had a different plan. The letter sparked a desire in me to go see the college, resulting in that peace-filled flight to Portland that felt more like a homecoming than a first visit.

Jesus cleared all the obstacles to my attending college, including big financial barriers. The fall of 1996 found me a young seventeen-year-old freshman at Western Baptist College in Salem, Oregon. Great peace comes when we are living in the will of God. I do not say great ease, for the life of a Christ follower is rarely easy; but with obedience to the Father, it is a life marked by the Spirit's peace.

As I look back over the film of my life, I see with clarity how Whisper after Whisper guided me along His right paths for my life. I can see His intervention, protection, and deliverance. He said no to some prayers for which I desperately wanted a yes, but His no's ended up providing things eternally better. Relationships were restored when He moved my feet forward to forgive and be forgiven. Precious friendships were birthed from His divinely appointed crossing of paths.

One of those friendships is with my nearest and dearest comrade, my husband. Steve and I both ended up being transplanted to the Pacific Northwest after our high-school years together in California. He attended Walla Walla College in eastern Washington. Our friendship, which had begun when Jesus had crossed our paths on my fourteenth birthday, grew deeper for ten years before God unveiled the plan He'd put in place, before we were born, to unite Stephen Engelman and Lisa Winters as husband and wife. Steve remains my best earthly example of the love of Christ—a love without condition. In following the Whisper from Jesus to attend college in Oregon, I ended up only five hours from where Jesus took Steve to college. Now we have lived in the Northwest for almost fifteen of our seventeen years of marriage—the result of listening to His Whisper and then moving forward.

Jesus knew to seek His Father's voice before moving forward in choosing His twelve apostles (see Luke 6:12–13). As students of our beloved Rabbi, how much more should we take time to pray before making decisions, waiting on God for His answer. As we draw our focus to the Holy Spirit's presence within us, waiting with wholly surrendered hearts, His Whisper will direct our steps.

STRONGER TOGETHER: LED INTO FELLOWSHIP

As an introvert, I don't generally frequent large conferences or workshops. But the times I have said, "Yes, Lord," when the Spirit has nudged me to attend one has increased my awareness that obedience brings spiritual blessings. One such occasion took place at our local church when we lived in Southern California. When the women's ministry director announced a workshop on anxiety and depression, I felt the Holy Spirit's familiar nudge to sign up. I am so glad I did!

During the last part of the workshop, the workshop leaders opened up the microphone to the audience to ask questions. A young mom on the opposite side of the auditorium stood up and asked raw questions about the goodness of God, as her heavenly Father, in her time of intense pain. My heart sped up as the directive to go to this young woman came. When the workshop was over, I made my way to her, having no idea what I would say. But God usually has a way of taking over a conversation when we declare our complete insufficiency and plead, "Take over me, Lord!"

I waited a few minutes while two other women spoke with her. When they were finished talking, she turned questioning eyes to me, having no clue who I was. I introduced myself to her and explained that I was new to the church. Lacking any eloquence, I blurted out that my heart ached for her. I shared that while the women's ministry leaders were answering her question from the stage, I was sensing how deeply the Father loved her, that He was pleased by her seeking Him without holding back her truest feelings and thoughts. He wanted her questions, hurts, uncertainties—all of her! I hugged her and said, "It's okay not to be okay."

After our tears and hugs, she turned and introduced me to the two other women who had been talking to her. They invited me to join their Bible-study group that was starting up the following week. When I went to the Bible study, I met a dear sister in Christ with a deep love for Jesus, overflowing wisdom, and arms of love. She introduced me to a version of the Bible called the Tree of Life Version, put together by Jewish scholars. I have grown to love this version of the Bible! Reading familiar verses that use the names of "Adonai" and "Yeshua" for our God has been impactful for me. Blessings await our obedience to the Whisper within.

Being a part of the workshop reminded me of the strength and joy we receive when we gather with other believers. I have experienced it as well sitting barefoot in the grass at a park when I lived near another close friend in sunny California. With faces turned up to the sun, we experienced the warmth of friendship in Jesus as we poured out our hearts and prayed. When I gather with believers whose faces are radiant with the love of Christ, I see an outward manifestation of the Spirit filling us to overflowing.

We become stronger after worshiping together with our forever families at our local churches. We experience joy when we team up with one another to serve using the gifts bestowed on us by the Spirit. Francis Chan writes, "You are a part of something much bigger than yourself, something sacred. Through Jesus' sacrifice, you have been joined to His Church. Because of this, you are not only a part of God's sacred temple, but also a part of the heavenly community."[1]

In Ephesians Paul teaches about being joined together to become God's dwelling place:

You Gentiles are no longer strangers and foreigners. You are citizens along with all of God's holy people. You are members of God's family. Together, we are his house, built on the foundation of the apostles and the prophets. And the cornerstone is Christ Jesus himself. We are carefully joined together in him, becoming a holy temple for the Lord. Through him you Gentiles are also being made part of this dwelling where God lives by his Spirit. (Eph. 2:19–22)

We are each living stones joining together to form this dwelling place for God (see 1 Pet. 2:5)!

The day after I graduated college, I ran my first marathon down the Avenue of the Giants in the Redwoods of Northern California. These enormous trees rising more than two hundred feet actually have a shallow root depth in comparison to their height. Their strength to weather storms comes from their roots growing together, intertwined, even fused! We are joined through the Spirit to God our Father, Jesus the beloved Son, and a *huge* forever family!

Hebrews 11, known as the faith chapter, is followed in Hebrews 12 by a description of the great cloud of witnesses. I enjoy reading biographies of spiritual giants of the faith who have now joined that great cloud of witnesses. Their courage and perseverance strengthen my faith.

I also take note of believers today, a few years ahead of me on the path of life, who are following hard after Jesus in the face of adversity. I used to shake my head in wonder at how they continued in full-time ministry while suffering immense personal heartache. The Spirit taught me that He will be strong in me too. I praise the Lord and continue to fervently intercede for them, but I no longer have to ask, "*How* do they do that?"

I can read Galatians 2:8 and resonate with Paul: the same God at work in Peter was at work in Paul, and He is at work in believers everywhere, including *me*. They sought after God with their whole, surrendered hearts, living Spirit-filled lives. We can too! We can ask, seek, and knock (see Matt. 7:7). We can confess and surrender, knowing that it is the same God working in each of us to give us the desire and the power to do what pleases Him who worked in them (see Phil. 2:13). We can receive strengthening joy as we listen to Holy Spirit-filled preachers who are unafraid to speak the truth of God's Word in its entirety.

When we witness believers all around the world serving the poor, ministering to the sick, and enduring affliction, our joyful response can be, "*Wow*, God, *You* are powerful beyond what I can ask or imagine and powerfully at work within and through us. Thank You, Father" (see Eph. 3:20–21)! We are always stronger together!

WHO TOLD YOU THAT?

Quite some time after I was diagnosed with cancer, I received a powerful Whisper that now shapes the daily decisions I make. It came after I was considering the question "Who told you that?" Doctors told me multiple times that I would die from an incurable type of lymphoma. But Jesus has ordered my steps, and I am still here today.

The Spirit turned this question into a Whisper, "*Who told you that?*" to unveil the hurting places in my heart where negative words had taken root. I had allowed the low statistics of survival that had been given to me years ago to close the door to any thought of a long-term future here on Earth. Each birthday celebration for my sweet children was overshadowed by wondering if I would be here for the next. Even my daily decisions sometimes included a voice that kept bringing those words of the doctor back to me.

And so it went until I surrendered everything—my life and the questions. The Spirit asked me to take the doctor's words to the throne and remember that I have been crucified with Christ and that I no longer live but Christ lives in me. The life I live in the body I live by faith in the Son of God, who loved me and gave Himself for me (see Gal. 2:20). Proverbs 4:23 cautions us to guard our hearts, for it determines the course of our lives. The New King James Version says, "Keep your heart with all diligence, for out of it spring the issues of life" (Prov. 4:23). My favorite version is, "Above all else, guard your heart, for everything you do flows from it" (Prov. 4:23, NIV).

When we dwell in the Word with the Word, we begin to have the mind of Christ and view life from a divine perspective. Even when we face a physician's declaration of a disease being incurable, we can choose to receive the word that God has spoken, "All things are possible" (Matt. 19:26, NKJV), and this leaves the door to miraculous healing wide open. Our behavior follows our beliefs. We live defeated lives when we lose sight of "with God all things are possible."

One day I will be at home with Jesus and have sight for my faith. Until that day I desire my steps to travel in the way of the righteous, like the first gleam of dawn that shines ever brighter until the full light of day (see Prov. 4:18–19)! By faith in God's Word, I can live the abundant life for which Jesus died and rose again. This means living with complete trust in the days numbered for me and spending each of those days vibrantly loving Jesus and loving others. Knowing that I am upheld by the Creator of the universe to live out the days He ordained for me before time began has enabled me to walk in freedom rather than fear. God's voice alone has authority over me.

Who told me that? *God* did!

How Will This Change Us?

"You will be changed by what you step toward." This Whisper was powerfully driven into my soul through my pastor at our local church. It has directed my steps when I have been presented with daily decision making in parenting or choosing commitments.

We will be changed by the people we spend time with and the activities we choose to engage in. Will these things pull us closer to God? Do they align with our prayerful priorities? My sin nature, Mrs. Self, loves to lure my steps away from the Word of God toward lesser things. The Lord reminds me, *"My dear daughter, stay away from anything that takes My place in your heart"* (see 1 John 5:21). The Lord will use His gentle voice within us to steer us away from things that would harm our communion with Him and to move us toward His plan and purpose for our lives. He created us to fulfill the good things He planned for us to do before we were even born (see Eph. 2:10)!

When we step closer to Jesus, not only will it change us, but it will also produce a response in us! We should ask ourselves, "How will this encounter I just had with God change me?" When Paul was on the road to Damascus, he met Jesus and fell to his knees, blinded. Trembling and astonished, he said, "Lord, what do You want me to do?" (Acts 9:6, NKJV).

Sometimes we will feel a quickening within us when we read a Bible verse. This happened to me during my journey through Joshua when I read, "Choose today whom you will serve" (Josh. 24:15). What followed was the Spirit within me whispering, *"Choose Me."* My soul leaped in response to this Whisper from God's Word to make a choice. I began to scribble earnestly in my journal that I would choose Jesus. "I choose light. I choose faithfulness. I choose to persevere when I do not understand, and often I don't. I choose my heavenly inheritance, my Father's everlasting blessings, over man's temporal praise."

As my pastor often declares, "I will choose my course, because I want the overwhelming presence of Jesus in my life!" With my whole heart, I can say, "I choose You, Father. I want Your will, Your way. I want to live the life of the blessed! Change me, Lord!"

PONDERING THE PATHS OF OUR FEET

When I read through Isaiah this last year, I found myself stuck on the words "Woe to those who go to Egypt but didn't ask God's advice" (see Isa. 30:2). This has been a yellow caution light at every intersection of my life blinking, "Warning: ask God first!" Isaiah teaches us to look to the Holy One of Israel rather than relying on horses and trusting in chariots (see Isa. 31:1). Instead of taking the counsel of others who devise plans that are not from the Holy Spirit, we must go to the Lord who is wonderful in counsel and excellent in guidance (see Isa. 28:29; 30:1).

"Ponder the path of your feet, and let all your ways be established" (Prov. 4:26, NKJV). At every place of uncertainty in decisions we face, we can pray for the Spirit to cause scriptures that are relevant to our current situation to *leap* off the pages of the Word. We can plead with Jesus for a word from the Word. Jesus longs to guide our decisions, comfort us in our pain, and speak to our earnest prayer requests. I love to comb through Proverbs 3 and 4 when I am in need of wisdom or a heart reset. During my most recent trip through these chapters, the word "peace" jumped out to me. God promises us peace when our hearts keep His commandments (see Prov. 3:1–2).

We can easily mistake our own thoughts for the leading of the Whisper within if we stray from grounding ourselves in the Word daily. Comparing the Word with the Word protects us from misinterpreting Scripture when we feel unsure of the Spirit's Whisper. Psalm 33:6 connects God's spoken word with His breath, or Whisper: "The LORD merely spoke, and the heavens were created. He breathed the word, and all the stars were born." The Word *and* the Spirit brought the universe into existence, and both sustain it. The same is true in our lives. We are sustained and led by the spoken word of God and the Spirit breathing life into us. Hunger for both the Word and the Spirit together will raise the volume of God's voice in our lives.

Excitement fills me when the written Word leaps to life and validates something that the Spirit has impressed on my heart. Faith comes by hearing, and hearing by the Word. Reading the written Word of God increases our faith. It grows our capacity to act on what He has written.

Surrendering to the Lord as we ponder our lives' paths is like putting the tires on a car into alignment. When we hold onto things He has asked us to release, we become misaligned, which makes it hard for us to stay on the road He appoints us to. Prone to wander, we live in daily need of the Spirit's alignment—our wills becoming His will, our paths His path. "I will instruct you and teach you in the way you should go; I will counsel you with my loving eye on you" (Ps. 32:8, NIV).

TAKE AN EXTRA BOOK!

One of my favorite Whispers that resulted in big smiles took place when Luke and I went out to celebrate the release of my first book, *Meet My Medical Director: Navigating Cancer's Storm*. Steve and I had had our own celebration, but we decided that ten-year-old Luke and I should have a special night together honoring his hard work in putting together the promotional video for the book. As Luke and I prepared to make the one-hour drive to Newport Beach, California, I clearly heard the Lord prompt me through His Whisper within to go back to the house and get an extra book to take with us. I had no idea why. I told Luke, "Buddy, let's see what Jesus does with this book!"

Luke and I enjoyed a delightful dinner together seated outdoors by the fireplace at True Food Kitchen in Newport Beach. I was shocked when the waitress assigned to our table remembered me from six years prior! Steve had taken me out for dinner at the same place toward the end of my first round of cancer treatment at a nearby integrative medical center. This waitress had just been talking to her children about our family, wondering if I was okay. Then I walked in the very next day!

We talked over the years that had passed and God's goodness. I told her that we were celebrating the completion of the book when I stopped mid-sentence. "Oh! We have a book especially for you!" Luke thought of it at the same moment and asked, "Momma, can I go get the book from the car and give it to her?"

Jesus has come through in spectacular ways so many times for me that I now just smile and know that He is up to something, even if I can't see it just yet. If it means turning my car around to go get what He says to get, so be it!

LOVE ENDURES THROUGH EVERY CIRCUMSTANCE

The horizon of a new decade was in sight. In reflecting on the road of life behind and before us, I noticed that the circumstances in view remained mountainous. Seasons of difficulty intensified my longing to lean in close to Jesus. Looking upon a new year brought with it an opportunity for reflection and renewal. So in December 2019, in preparation for a new year and a new decade, I traveled through Dallas Willard's *Renovation of the Heart*. It pointed me to a list of Scripture passages showing what apprentices of Jesus are to look like.[2]

The Holy Spirit prompted me to step closer into the life of our Messiah in 2020 by reading the Gospels and studying the passages Dallas Willard had recommended. He put it on my heart to notice as much as I could about Jesus, taking special note of how the Lord had spent time, the numerous accounts of His tenderness and compassion, and His character and decisions. I was to cultivate such an awareness of His presence that I could receive His encouragement and teachings as if He were right in front of me so that I could look deep into His eyes when He told me that I was valuable to Him (see Matt. 6:26).

One of the passages from Dallas Willard's list of scriptures recently rescued me from being trapped in momma discouragement. When challenges with my children arise, God's Word directs my steps. When I woke up one day stuck in parenting perplexities, 1 Corinthians 13 "happened" to be the next passage on the list for me to study:

Love is patient and kind. Love is not jealous or boastful or proud or rude. It does not demand its own way. It is not irritable, and it keeps no record of being wronged. It does not rejoice about injustice but rejoices whenever the truth wins out. Love never gives up, never loses faith, is always hopeful, and endures through every circumstance. (1 Cor. 13:4–7)

The Spirit did what He is famous for in my life: He used a gentle squeeze on my heart to move me toward repentance, helping me realize that I had been parenting out of my sin nature rather than out of the Spirit of love within. He caused the words "love is not irritable" to leap to life in my soul. I grew excited to think of what this kind of love might do in my relationships with my growing children. A love that *wasn't* irritable? Didn't keep a record of wrong? Sign me up!

The year 2020 dawned brightly as I officially entered the apprenticeship of Jesus Christ with my list of Scripture passages from Dallas Willard. Jesus is love (see 1 John 4:8). His love in us is the love that "endures through every circumstance" (1 Cor. 13:7). Taped onto my prayer wall was this pledge: "Jesus, I dedicate my life to You as Your apprentice. Teach me as You taught Your disciples when You walked the earth how to live Your life of love." As a family, we committed to a 2020 journey through the Gospels at family dinners to have Jesus teach us His ways.

One night Sammy J set some of his salmon on an extra plate for Jesus to join us at dinner. "Jesus likes fish, Momma!"

This boy loves the red letters in the Bible. Sammy J often brings his Bible to my bedside in the mornings and pleads, "Please, Momma, read me the red letters. I want to hear Jesus talk to me!" Recently he opened his Bible to Matthew 7 and asked me to read verses 7 through 11:

> Keep on asking, and you will receive what you ask for. Keep on seeking, and you will find. Keep on knocking, and the door will be opened to you. For everyone who asks, receives. Everyone who seeks, finds. And to everyone who knocks, the door will be opened.
>
> You parents—if your children ask for a loaf of bread, do you give them a stone instead? Or if they ask for a fish, do you give them a snake? Of course not! So if you sinful people know how to give good gifts to your children, how much more will your heavenly Father give good gifts to those who ask him.

Jesus used Sammy J to remind me how much God loves me and desires to give us good gifts, so I was to keep asking, keep seeking, and keep knocking!

One of the Whispers that came as I worked my way through Willard's list studying the life of Jesus was to pursue a lighthearted home. Steve and I realized after six years of traveling through difficulties that we had forgotten that Jesus was the One packing our trials, on His own back. Our children needed to experience the happiness of Jesus within our home—to watch their parents live under the gentle and easy yoke of a Savior who promises to carry our burdens.

Trust lightens and brightens every atmosphere, beginning within our own souls and radiating into our homes and communities. Our family has been stepping with the Spirit toward creating a lighthearted home by choosing to be in nature together more often, playing hide-and-seek and board games, increasing laughter, and taking more family trips to the park. Jesus opened a door for the girls to receive their dream of trying a ballet class after four years of asking. Watching them delight in it has given me momma joy.

Taking a leap of trust into this new place was done only through the work of the Holy Spirit within, who reminds us to stay in our todays. This is the day the Lord has made, and we will be glad and rejoice in it (see Ps. 118:24)! Studying the life of Jesus has increased my desire to trust Him in all things. Jesus, Immanuel, God with us. His love in us. Always!

Unique Assignments

The evergreen trees towered high with gigantic maple trees growing alongside them, shading the bike trail ahead. It was a gorgeous Fourth of July morning and our very first family-of-six bike ride! Gazing ahead, my smile grew wider as I watched each of my five family members riding single file ahead of me—Daddy in the lead and Momma the caboose with four sets of growing legs peddling quickly under the canopy of trees in a forest thick with ferns. The Whisper from within came: "*This day happened because I changed the course of your life.*"

I pondered that in prayer as I rewound the film of my life back to January 2014, remembering when the doctor at our local hospital where I had first been diagnosed wanted me to immediately enter aggressive chemo. The Lord had put His hand in the way in the form of a huge red stop sign in my heart. Through fervent prayer, Steve and I had both known that the path they recommended was not the one the Holy Spirit desired us to take. Jesus directed our steps down a gentler path that has been marked by His provision and peace for every step.

In my book *Meet My Medical Director: Navigating Cancer's Storm*, I talk more in depth about the numerous ways Jesus has guided me through cancer's storm as my Medical Director. I would have been lost in a sea of confusion without His trusted voice through His written Word and His counseling Spirit within me. Upon completion of that book in 2018, the story was not over. While I have remained in remission now for four years, our family continues to travel through trials, experiencing desperation for all of Jesus—to hear His voice, to know that He holds our tears and carries our burdens.

Each of us is on unique assignment from the Almighty to be lived out through the power of the Spirit within. The Lord may take us on unexpected paths that may include opposing voices. The secret to not growing weary and losing heart is keeping our eyes fixed on Jesus in this race we are asked to run (see Heb. 12:1–3).

When my steps become shaky and the future looks unclear, Jeremiah 29:11 has been a Whisper to me again and again since my cancer diagnosis in December 2013: "*'I know the plans I have for you,' says the LORD. 'They are plans for good and not for disaster, to give you a future and a hope.'*" God's plans are for us to step forward into unshakable hope—the arms of Jesus Himself. The truly abundant life is like a waterfall in the spring that pours forth God's goodness and love into the lives of those around us. We do not need to muster up the good that we pour into others; we receive it from Christ Himself.

When Jesus walked the earth, He gave us His footprints so we can follow His ways of love. The best gift we can give to other wounded and tired hearts all around us is to stay on the path marked out for us. We can allow the Holy Spirit to guide every detail of our life, trusting moment by moment in the *God* who still authors miracles, still rescues, and still sustains. As we create quiet spaces by fellowshipping with Jesus in His Words through His Spirit, we experience deep rest in His Creator's love as His Whisper directs our every step.

⸺ *Pray It In* ⸺

Give ear to my words, oh Lord; consider my meditation. Give heed to the voice of my cry, my King and my God. To You I will pray. My voice You will hear in the morning, oh Lord; in the morning I will direct it to You, and I will look up (see Ps. 5:1–3). As I revere *You*, Adonai, You will show me the path I should choose (see Ps. 25:12). I belong to You, God. You hold my right hand and guide me with Your counsel, leading me to a glorious destiny (see Ps. 73:23–24). Make Your way straight before my face (see Ps. 5:7–8). The plans of my heart belong to me, but my tongue's answers are from You, Adonai. I commit all I do to You, Adonai, and I know that You will make my plans succeed. My heart may plan my course, but You direct my steps (see Prov. 16:1–3, 9).

Jesus, thank You for taking hold of me today. I rest in Your love.

12

WHISPERS
RENEW PERSPECTIVES

I climbed into the Uber car, curious about the driver wearing a flat cap with a smile stretching from ear to ear. Excited for my morning trip up to Seattle to be with my momma on her seventieth birthday, I settled into the back seat on our way to the train station to take in the last glimpses of the gorgeous fall season coloring Portland.

The hip-hop music in the car caught my attention as I caught phrases of God's Word mixed in with the beat. I bravely asked the driver what kind of music it was. With a beautiful Nigerian accent, he told me it was called prison worship. Oh, the goodness of God! A man who loved Jesus was driving me to my train!

One question after another spilled out as we recognized God's handiwork in crossing our paths so we could share the joy of Jesus that had been birthed in adversity. During that forty-nine-minute drive to the train station, God's Word bounced back and forth like a ping-pong ball between the front and back seat, strengthening faith and exploding joy into the atmosphere. I could not stop grinning.

I am still smiling as I write this. My Uber driver grew up in Nigeria. He knew well the faces of suffering. With fervor he shared with me how the excruciating hardships his family had endured had grown his faith. With contagious thankfulness and excitement, he declared, "Jesus is the only way a poor man, a man who is nothing, a man such as me," he said pointing to himself, "could be so rich!"

From his holy-laughter-filled voice, one could not guess that he labored so diligently to earn money simply to send every dollar he could to his family in Nigeria to sustain their lives. With such joy radiating from his whole being, I would never have guessed that he had gone five years without seeing his family. Scripture poured out from him as we made our way to the train station, strengthening my soul (see Ps. 138:3). I sensed God's smile upon us as He delighted in bringing two of His children together to glorify Him on that fall Portland day.

The gift of extra time, due to thick morning traffic, allowed story after story of God's faithfulness to rise in worship from the Uber car that day. Whispers from within me rose up: "*Peace is within you, My daughter. I am your peace. Peace doesn't come from an easy life but from having a surrendered, unhurried soul.*" My sight grew clearer that day as His Whispers renewed my perspective. I saw how God had raised up this sweet soul through unfathomable hardships to be His spokesman in an Uber car ministry in Portland, Oregon.

"Yes, Father, I hear You. Hard times sometimes are Your goodness in disguise—You working behind what we can see to make us more like Your Son, and not just for our earthly days, but for eternity with You. Give us eyes to see, Lord, ears to hear, and hearts to love!" What I experienced on my Uber car ride that crisp fall morning was the Spirit returning my soul's vision from looking at my troubling circumstances to looking upon my Savior.

When Being Who We Are Feels Hard

On certain days I have tearfully expressed to Steve, "Husband, sometimes it's just *so* hard to be me!" On one of these days, as I melted into the worn spot on my prayer-closet floor, the Whisper came: "*You are fearfully and wonderfully made*" (see Ps. 139:14). God reminded me that I have a part in His mega-story of life that only I can play. I am to stay true to who He created me to be.

I have a brain that absorbs information at an alarming rate and a heart so tender that it often hurts. While this can be a rough combination, I have experienced God using it for His kingdom so many times that I officially surrendered my questions such as "Why was I made this way?" and accepted His declaration that indeed I am *wonderfully* made. On the days when I hurt, He holds me. It's just me and Jesus. I can sing with Him, pour out my heart in raw honesty, or say nothing at all, and yet He hears me.

The most important thing is not what we do but who we become. Jesus gently reminded me that a rainbow is stunning because of the contrast of its colors. Each of us with our unique quirks, giftings, and personalities join as one in the Spirit to shine His Creator love brightly and beautifully into this storm-darkened world.

Remembering Our Purpose

Why were we created?

God created us for His pleasure (see Rev. 4:11). He created us for His glory (see Isa. 43:7). We were designed to be diffusers: "Thanks be to God, who in Christ always leads us in triumphal procession, and through us spreads the fragrance of the knowledge of him everywhere" (2 Cor. 2:14, ESV).

I have placed diffusers for essential oils throughout my home. They all exist to improve the environment, but their purposes change with the type of oil I put inside them. Some are for fragrance, cleaning, or relaxation. Others help with allergies or colds. Others help us fall asleep at night. Each of us is God's vessel. We are filled with different "oils" but all created for the same purpose: to diffuse "the fragrance of His knowledge [Christ's] in every place" (2 Cor. 2:14, NKJV).

God may send us to serve in hospitals, prisons, remote villages, homeless shelters, workplaces, schools, grocery stores, or local churches. He may have us diffuse His love primarily within our homes. Some diffuse as extroverts, others as introverts. Some hold roles that we perceive as big, others jobs that seem invisible, for now. "The time is coming when everything that is covered up will be revealed, and all that is secret will be made known to all" (Luke 12:2). One of my favorite things that Steve says is that those who have been least here on Earth, in roles like faithful gospel-sharing janitors, will be great in heaven. "Many who are the greatest now will be least important then, and those who seem least important now will be the greatest then" (Matt. 19:30). Amen!

God always leads us in triumph (see 2 Cor. 2:14), which means that we are victorious in Jesus wherever we go! We are on the winning side! Knowing that my life's circumstances are by God's sovereign allowance for the furthering of His kingdom helps me trust Him in all things, with all people. Contentment fosters joy.

Examples in the Bible of those who endured hardships give us the gift of hindsight, which provides divine perspective on our own trials. For example, we know from the life of Job that *God* sets the limits, not Satan. God decides, always. Much suffering came to Job, but Satan was not allowed to take Job's life (see Job 2:6).

I have received the Whisper a couple times, when praying in the midst of a valley, to *"consider the heavenly courts"* (see Job 1:6). When I consider what may be happening in the heavenly courts, I remember that there is an accuser. He would like me to be frozen by doubt, discouraged and defeated. The Whisper to "*remember the unseen*" has renewed my perspective repeatedly (see 2 Kings 6:16–17). Our spiritual battle with evil is real, but so too are the angels who minister to us and defend us. The Lord of angel armies is always present with us.

Another example that clarifies our perspectives is seen in the severe trial in the garden of Gethsemane, when Jesus asked His Father if there could be another way besides dying on the cross. Yet with immense eternal purpose, Jesus was led to the cross. We read of this purpose in Hebrews: Jesus, for the joy set before Him, endured the cross and despised the shame. Now He has the best perspective of all on His heavenly throne (see Heb. 12:2). His message from the garden powerfully speaks divine perspective into the blackest of nights. As we cry hard tears, we can say, "Father, have *Your* way with me!"

Nothing is ever wasted with our heavenly Father. Nothing is missed by His watchful eye. Perhaps that is a painful truth at times, but it is a truth that anchors us in the hope that will not disappoint at eternity's shore. "You keep track of all my sorrows. You have collected all my tears in your bottle. You have recorded each one in your book" (Ps. 56:8).

Often it is those who have spent agonizing hours in their own gardens of Gethsemane who become safe messengers to speak about God's presence and goodness in the midst of pain to those in desperate need of a holding hug rather than a piercing platitude. We learn from their experiences about how God's character was revealed to them during their nights in the garden of Gethsemane—answers to their own John the Baptist moments of wondering why Jesus was not acting in the way they expected.

After John the Baptist was imprisoned, he sent a couple of his disciples to ask Jesus, "Lord, should I look for another?" (see Luke 7:19). Perhaps he was perplexed, having been stuck in Herod's prison, as to whether the Messiah, the One who saves, had truly come. His captivity was, well, unexpected. The answer from His beloved Messiah was for John to know that "the blind receive sight, the lame walk, those who have leprosy are cleansed, the deaf hear, the dead are raised, and the good news is proclaimed to the poor" (Luke 7:22, NIV). Yes, Jesus was John the Baptist's beloved Messiah, and He is ours!

It is a hard but eternally beautiful truth that *God carried the life of John the Baptist to its intended completion.* John the Baptist died in his thirties, but he lived a spiritually full life, finishing all the good works that God had prepared in advance for him to do (see Eph. 2:10; Phil. 1:6). His role in God's mega-story was complete.

JESUS AS OUR TEACHER

Jesus was an incredible teacher. I love to immerse myself in the red letters recorded in the Bible spoken by our Rabbi. What power in His words! We have the opportunity to be taught by the Messiah and have our thoughts shaped by His teaching. We are transformed into new people as God changes the way we think (see Rom. 12:2).

I am experiencing a lighter step now in my forties as I allow my beliefs to be shaped by the teaching of Jesus. I am loved by Him just as I am—an introvert who loves people yet needs quiet as a regular rhythm in my day. The quiet equips me to give to others more rather than less. Jesus has changed my thinking from "What is wrong with me?" to "Thank You, Jesus, for teaching me that You have made me this way for Your glory!"

We live in a culture consumed with the practice of emptying our minds. This type of meditation—to think about nothing— is not the way of Jesus. Our journeys to increase in Christlike character require us to think long on Jesus—to put on His life, His love, His thinking. We must meditate on His words and His ways as recorded in the perfect Word of God. This is far different from

Eastern meditation, in which the goal is to empty. Biblical meditation is filling. By it we take in God's words and assimilate them into who we are becoming. As we think long on Jesus, we fall further in love. As we love Him more, we think on Him more. This cycle continues, forming us bit by bit into the image of Jesus Christ.

Thinking on Jesus is like turning on a light switch in the dark room of our minds. It doesn't work well to fight against all the thoughts we know we shouldn't be fixating on, does it? But what happens when we are in a dark room and we reach over and hit the light switch? As light floods the room, darkness is no longer present. So it is with our minds. God's Word is the light. As we dedicate time to taking God into our minds through His Word, He fills our thoughts with His light. We then dwell upon His very presence and His love. Life then becomes not so much about "Don't do this," "Don't do that" as a natural outcome of holy living due to our time spent meditating on Jesus and His words.

We are constantly being changed. The question is, what changes are taking place in us? We *will* be changed by what we take in through our eyes and our ears. Reading God's Word and listening to music that points us to Jesus both serve to increase our hunger for God and His ways. Our decision to choose what Jesus would choose brings honor to His name.

This is true as well of the people with whom we cultivate close friendships, for we will become like those we spend time with. While it is our joyful ministry to be ambassadors for Christ, carrying His good news to all those around us, Jesus teaches us by example that our inner circle of friends should be wholehearted Christ followers. Often just taking note of what those around us are pursuing, what they like to talk about, and how they spend their time can reveal the hunger of their souls. "As iron sharpens iron, so a friend sharpens a friend" (Prov. 27:17). I am eternally grateful for the dear friends around me who sharpen my hunger for Jesus.

WHAT DO OUR LIVES DECLARE ABOUT GOD?

I have a pink Post-it note up on my prayer wall with the question "What does my life declare about God?" This question is one I return to when my eyes see only my problems and not my Savior. It helps me look beyond my hardships to the finish line, reminding me that the finish line is really only the starting line of eternity with my Beloved!

Once I make my safe arrival in the Celestial City, where a growing crowd of saints awaits with King Jesus, I will lose my opportunity to reach lost souls for the kingdom. I will no longer be able to encourage fellow believers to press on through trial in the strength of Christ. Today presents me with that opportunity for my life to declare *something* about God. What will that declaration be? What do I desire it to be? That life is hard, so— we should just give up? *No!*

I want others to know that Jesus is worth our perseverance. This includes persevering in prayer for things that we've been asking about for years, persevering in parenting, and persevering in making wise lifestyle decisions to be the best versions of ourselves that we can be. When we forge ahead of Him on our own ways, however, forgetting to cast the outcome of our circumstances upon His Savior shoulders, we can fall back into the arms of Jesus and renew our declaration that we won't give up on seeking Him.

Our choices have weight and hold potential for eternal value. Sometimes I tell my children that I just heard a *clink* in the piggy bank awaiting them in heaven when I catch them being kind or helpful. Just this morning my ball-of-energy youngest child, Sammy J, was carrying my dishes for me and looked up with a grin and said "*Clink*" before he took them to the sink. One act in Jesus' name drops a "coin" into our eternal-reward piggy banks awaiting us upon our arrival in heaven.

May our lives declare with every choice to persevere in Jesus' name—that God is so worthy of all honor, all glory, and all praise, now and forevermore (see Rev. 5:12)!

CALL TO VISION

Early one morning Sammy J snuck quietly into my prayer closet while I was praying, plopped himself down in my lap, and asked if he could have prayer time with me. He pulled a quilt around us as tight as his five-year-old arms could manage, looked up at me, and asked, "Momma, what do you love about Jesus?"

Pulling his sweet self closer, I looked into his inquisitive eyes and realized that this was one of those rare moments when I had his complete attention! His eyes locked on mine, *really* wanting to know what I loved about Jesus! It was my call to vision for the day.

With quiet delight, I called to mind and spoke about my Savior: His patience, tenderness, gentle shepherd care; His love, His endless power; His authorship of anything He desired to speak into existence, miracles of all shapes and sizes, grace to deliver, grace to sustain. A short minute later, Sammy J popped off my lap and ran out of the closet, seemingly satisfied with my answer before I was even close to finishing.

When the difficulties we face become overwhelming, we can call to vision our Savior. We can bring the cross to mind, then the tomb, and then the stone being rolled away. We can strain to hear the voice of the risen Savior making His presence known to His disciples. We can feel the heat of their joy. We can experience the wind of Pentecost connecting us to God's very Spirit within. We can remember the promise of Matthew 16:27: "The Son of Man will come in the glory of His Father with His angels, and then He will reward each according to His works" (NKJV). He came, and He is coming again!

Every time we call to vision Jesus Christ in the midst of towering waves and choose to trust Him, it's a deposit into kingdom glory ahead! "I have set *ADONAI* always before me. Since He is at my right hand, I will not be shaken" (Ps. 16:8, TLV). We can *shout* for joy, for *God* defends us. He surrounds us with His favor as a shield (see Ps. 5:11–12). "The word of the LORD holds true, and we can trust everything he does" (Ps. 33:4).

GOD IS WATCHING OVER US

I rounded a corner on a trail at the mountain nature park by my house, lost in my thoughts about the constant heat of trial in my family. Suddenly before me stood a woman looking lost. She asked if I knew where the trailhead was. "Sure," I said. "I'm headed there myself. Let's go together!"

Her name was Maribella, and those minutes we spent walking together were a gift to my soul! Right before we parted at the top of the trail, she fixed her gaze right at my eyes, pointed with both hands up to the sky, and said, "*He* is watching over you!"

Her words came to mind the following morning in my prayer closet when the page I was to write on in my journal had this verse typed on the bottom: "Behold, the eye of the LORD is upon them that fear him, upon them that hope in his mercy" (Ps. 33:18, KJV). The heat of trial is real, but the presence of God reminds us that He is the fourth within our flames (see Dan. 3:24–25).

For those of us in the furnace of testing, rich fulfillment is ahead! "You, O God, have tested us; You have refined us as silver is refined. You brought us into the net; You laid affliction on our backs. You have caused men to ride over our heads; we went through fire and through water; but You brought us out to rich fulfillment" (Ps. 66:10–12, NKJV).

SIFTED AS WHEAT

During lunchtime on a regular at-home schooling day, my oldest daughter, Ellie Joy, declared in her sweet, factual way, "Momma,

I read my Bible today." A smile settles in my soul each time my children run to me and report that they are having their own Bible times.

"What did you read, sweetie?" I asked.

"I read Job 1," Ellie replied.

Wow, I thought. *Light reading for a newly turned nine-year-old!* "What did you think of Job 1, Ellie?"

"Momma, God let Satan mess with Job and his children."

When she spoke this, the Whisper came immediately from within me: "*Yes, you are being messed with too, sifted as wheat. I am strong in you.*" Three times the Whisper came. Sometimes that happens when the immediate response in my soul is a questioning, "Lord?" He affirmed to me twice that I was being sifted as wheat and promised that He would be strong in me.

That night, still deeply impacted by the realization of the intense wheat-sifting season I was going through, I prayed and fasted in my closet for the Spirit's filling. After two hours, the Spirit led me to wash my face, go downstairs, set the table, and eat with Steve. It seemed odd to me since I had committed to fasting for the night, but obedience always brings joy, so down the stairs I went! When Steve returned home from dropping the kids off at Awana club, he found a light dinner on the table, a candle lit, and a wife bursting with restored joy. We had forty minutes together in prayer, Scripture reading, and conversation.

That night Luke was struck with a sudden high fever, and Steve left for a business trip soon after. Jesus gifted us that night to strengthen our souls!

CHRIST, OUR PRICELESS INHERITANCE

While Steve was away on his business trip for a few days, I had a crying date while hidden between the doors of my fridge. I had hit emotional exhaustion at five that afternoon and was missing my husband's evening rescue so I could have some time alone.

While attempting to fix the kids' dinner, I had burst into tears behind the protection of those fridge doors.

After I drained my available tears, I wiped my face and returned to my mothering. A Whisper from 1 Peter came to hold me up during the hours that followed: *"There is a wonderful joy ahead. These trials are going to make your faith shine. I am keeping you safe"* (see 1 Pet. 1:5–7). I was safe with my Father. My inheritance was safe. My future was secure. My trials couldn't touch it; they could only deepen the beauty that I will have when Jesus comes.

The joy is in the watching and in the working while we watch. Whatever our circumstances, as followers of Jesus Christ, we can live with great expectation! Praise be to God, the Father of our Lord Jesus Christ! It's because of His incredible mercy that we have been born again and have this priceless inheritance kept safe for us in heaven, totally beyond the horrid change and decay of our current world (see 1 Pet. 1:3–5)!

God's Word is like the trail-map signs all over the nature park by our home. For my younger three children, the trail there is a *long* hike. What keeps them going in the right direction and excited for the journey is glimpsing a trail map ahead. Their tiredness vanishes as their legs pump joyously toward the next sign. They see how far they've come and how close their destination is. They are reassured that we are not lost! This is like our Christian journey—we run to the trail map of God's Word and have our perspective renewed!

On one of these hikes, Steve met us at the end of the trail with arms wide open. Each of the children sprinted toward him on weary legs as soon as they caught sight of their daddy. We too have a Daddy waiting for us. Home is not too far!

> Be truly glad. There is wonderful joy ahead, even though you must endure many trials for a little while. These trials will show that your faith is genuine. It is being tested as fire tests and purifies gold—though your faith is far more

precious than mere gold. So when your faith remains strong through many trials, it will bring you much praise and glory and honor on the day when Jesus Christ is revealed to the whole world. (1 Pet. 1:6–7)

Peter declares it to be *so* wonderful that even the angels are eagerly watching these things happen (see 1 Pet. 1:12)!

In Titus 2:12–13, we are instructed on how to live in this evil world with wisdom, devotion, and righteousness *while* looking forward with hope to that glorious day when Jesus will be revealed. Paul, writing to Titus, gave the same instruction that Peter gave us: we must find our energy for today's kingdom work through keeping the eyes of our souls fixed on the promised coming of Jesus. Every little deposit we make into our kingdom accounts stirs up a song of celebration in the courts above. It matters. The enemy wants us to think that our choices to trust Jesus in the small moments don't matter, but our choices to trust bring Him honor and glory.

God *is* who He says He is. He will do what He says He will do. I get excited "God bumps" everywhere just imagining the glorious unfolding ahead!

Taking the Long View

A few summers ago, a friend of mine went with her husband to hike the challenging Inca Trail up to Machu Picchu in Peru. The pictures she sent me were stunning. She declared that the spectacular view was worth hiking the grueling trail. In those moments when she was tempted to turn back, she brought to her mind the many feet that had climbed this trail before her and made it to the top. She kept a long view of the beauty that awaited her.

The trails of life can be difficult, hot, sweaty, long, and, at times, discouraging. But hard times are opportunities. They give us chances to walk by faith toward what we cannot see—the top of our Machu Picchus—as the Spirit is within us, beside us, ahead of us, and behind us. Every moment we choose to stay on the road less traveled, to choose Jesus over ease, the weight of glory increases.

Steve and I daily have the opportunity to model to our children the cycle of mistakes, forgiveness, renewal, grace, and perseverance. The kids have a front-row seat to watch us, in our imperfections, seek Jesus with all our hearts. It is my fervent desire to see Luke, Ellie, Gracie, and Sammy J love Jesus with all their hearts and walk with Him all their days.

In the hard stuff of life, when we make it to the top, we will be able to turn and strengthen our brothers with the same comfort others gave us in our own long hikes. It is those who *know* heavy trials who can best come alongside others who are in difficult circumstances. The glory awaiting us increases each time we say *yes* to Jesus, *yes* to hope, *yes* to one more step with Him, *yes* to loving Him, *yes* to trying again after a failure as we live freely under the blood of Jesus. All testing has its boundaries, and God's Spirit in us gives us perseverance that will finish its work in us so that we can be mature and complete, lacking nothing (see James 1:2–4).

Taking the long view today means seeing with our soul eyes our own Machu Picchus. Eternity's shore awaits. The glory will be stunning.

WE ARE IMMORTAL UNTIL OUR WORK IS DONE

I was reading Andrew Murray's biography by Leona Choy and had a giant Whisper leap off one of the letters that his wife, Emma, wrote: "*I am immortal til my work is done!*" Here is more of Emma's heart: "The only tinge of sadness I have, though I would not wish it otherwise, is that his [Andrew Murray's] deep earnestness and feeling for the matters of God so often exhaust his physical strength and remind me that he is human and life is uncertain. Yet I know that 'man is immortal til his work is done,' and I pray he may be long spared to be useful in his day and generation."[1]

"Yes, Lord!" I prayed. A desire for my life to be long spared and to be useful in my day and generation soared within me. I too experience physical exhaustion that seems to be chronic, but my heart yearns to see our generation rise up as people who recognize that they are unconditionally loved by Jesus. Relief ran through me when I read about my life being immortal until my work is done. Such freedom from worry is found in those words of truth!

Think about it! God may ask us to take the gospel to a remote tribe known for war or to an unstable country where churches are underground. He may sovereignly allow chronic illness, broken relationships, and other trials that look like dark tunnels without an end in sight. But nothing, absolutely nothing, can change the number of days ordained for us. In a world that shouts self-care as the focus of our lives, we must remember that it's *God's* care that brings true rest of soul. We are immortal until our work is done! Our life is completely under God's authority.

Ultimately, we will find our perspectives renewed when we rest quietly in Jesus with the simple knowledge that we are in Him and He is in us. We have this treasure, the light of the glory of Jesus, within our earthen vessels so that all may know "that the excellence of the power may be of God and not of us. We are hard-pressed on every side, yet not crushed; we are perplexed, but not in despair; persecuted, but not forsaken; struck down, but not destroyed" (2 Cor. 4:7–9, NKJV). We can choose, as Moses did, to keep our sights on Jesus. Moses kept right on going by keeping his eyes on the one who is invisible (see Heb. 11:27).

Oh, to keep right on going, with our eyes on our Beloved until that glorious day when we are safely home *forever*! As our perspective is renewed by the beat of our Father's heart, His Whisper comes from within, *"All is well; you are loved. Rest in Me."*

—ᴄ *Pray It In* ᴄ—

Adonai, I call You to mind as I pray. You are a high tower in times of trouble (see Ps. 9:9)! Let Your Word penetrate my heart (see Prov. 4:21–22). Thank You for Your light shining in me, a fragile jar of clay, making it clear to everyone that my power is from You and not of myself. I am pressed on every side by troubles, but I am not crushed. I am perplexed but not driven to despair (see 2 Cor. 4:7–8). Your voice, Adonai, is over the waters (see Ps. 29:3). Bring Jesus into my view as I fix my eyes directly ahead (see Prov. 4:25)! I will never give up, Father, because as Your grace reaches more and more people, You will receive more and more glory (see 2 Cor. 4:15–16)!

Father, I thank You that my present trouble, which is but for a moment, is working for me an exceeding and eternal weight of glory. Holy Spirit, train my eyes not to look at the things that are seen but to bring my focus to the things that are unseen. For I know that the things that are seen are temporary, but the things that are not seen are eternal (see 2 Cor. 4:17–18).

Jesus, thank You for taking hold of me today. I rest in Your love.

CONCLUSION

Even though I am in my early forties, I still release a contented sigh each time I enter the doorway of my parents' home. It is not the residence of my childhood, for they have moved several times since I was a kid. It is simply them. They are my parents, my safe place. When I am sleeping in their home, my little-girl self says that there is no cause for concern. If there is a fire, my parents will take care of it. If there is a spider on the ceiling, they've got it.

How much more am I safe as I make my home with my heavenly Father, sheltered in His arms. My entire spiritual journey is spent as a child in my Father's kingdom. It is in childlike faith and absolute trust in His perfect parenting that I experience Sabbath, being at ease, throughout my entire being. My worries cannot stay when I am flooded by my Father's love. He speaks with infinite tenderness toward me, assuring me that I am accepted for who I am, His beloved daughter, not for what I do. Any good works

I do are simply the fruit of His Spirit. He gently reminds me that any affliction He has allowed me has been for my spiritual formation into Christlikeness and for greater kingdom good.

On that summer drive when I first heard His powerful Whisper within my soul, "*I love you. I love you. I love you*," it was an invitation. My heavenly Father, manifesting Himself to me, was inviting me to come closer, lean against Him, and to let go; to open up the doors to the deepest part of me for His healing love to enter; to be emptied so I could be filled. That car ride brought Romans 5:5 to life for me: "We know how dearly God loves us, because he has given us the Holy Spirit to fill our hearts with his love."

The human soul longs for true love. The greatest Whisper ever spoken was the "I love you" of Jesus when He died on the cross, bearing our sorrow, sins, and sickness: "God so loved the world that He gave His only begotten Son, that whoever believes in Him should not perish but have everlasting life" (John 3:16, NKJV). When we believe in our bones the love that Jesus has for us—that we are each His personal concern today—it gives us eyes to take in the long view. We see eternity's shore. We see the day when sorrow and sighing will flee. That vision gives us fervor to live victoriously *now* through the strength of the Whisper within.

The long view sees Jesus seated over the troubles we face today, with divine boundaries for our pain firmly in place. Through her long view of our Savior's love, Fanny Crosby wrote the words to "Blessed Assurance." Despite her blindness, she lived with her eyes looking up, her hands surrendered at her sides, holding onto nothing yet possessing everything (see 2 Cor. 6:10). When we fully submit to Jesus, we experience deep rest in our souls. In Jesus, our imperishable, unfading treasure, we are happy and blessed! Watching and waiting, always looking up, we will taste and see that He is God and that He is good. We can sing along with Fanny Crosby, filled with His goodness, lost in His love:

Perfect submission, perfect delight,
Visions of rapture now burst on my sight;
Angels descending, bring from above
Echoes of mercy, whispers of love.

Perfect Submission, all is at rest,
I in my Savior, am happy and blest
Watching and waiting, looking above
Filled with His goodness, lost in His love.

When our souls are lost in the love of our Savior, all truly *is* at rest. Striving stops. We declare with quiet rejoicing, "It is well with me. Father, I want Your will, Your way." Rooted in the vast love Jesus has for us, meditating on His Word day and night, we live victorious lives that bear fruit in every season.

When we are filled with the Spirit and put at rest by His love, then His strength, not our own, will powerfully fill us to do the work He calls us to. We will be ready to say, as Jesus did, "I will do all that the Father desires so that the world will know that I love the Father. Arise, let us be going" (see John 14:31). Jesus, knowing that He was loved by His Father, desired to obey His Father and walk in His will. He knew that His obedience would prove to the world His love for His Father. Knowing that His time was drawing near to climb up onto the cross, He loved to the end (see John 13:1).

When we know this love, it will produce a response in us: We will arise from doubt, discouragement, and uncertainty. We will arise from unbelief. We will arise from prisons, no longer chained by fear or addictions. We will arise from the lies that have sidelined us. We will arise from disappointments, shame, guilt, and regrets.

The gentle voice of Jesus, our Creator, speaks His Whisper to each of us today: "*I love you. I love you. I love you. Come to Me. Stay with Me. Rest in My love.*" As we remain at rest in our Creator's love through His Whisper within, we will become fountains of His living water for thirsty souls all around us who are looking for hope that doesn't disappoint and love that never ends.

Let us rest in Jesus' love and then follow the holy steps of our Beloved: "Arise, let us be going."

NOTES

Preface

1. According to Medical News Today, dopamine "plays a role in the brain's pleasure and reward center, and it drives many behaviors. . . . Higher levels of dopamine can lead to feelings of euphoria, bliss, and enhanced motivation and concentration. Therefore, exposure to substances and activities that increase dopamine can become addictive to some people" (Jamie Eske, "Dopamine and Serotonin: Brain Chemicals Explained," MedicalNewsToday, August 19, 2019, https://www.medicalnewstoday.com/articles/326090 [accessed July 13, 2020]). Praise "dopamine" refers to seeking pleasure from people's applause instead of resting in God's love for us.

Chapter 1: Creating Quiet Spaces

1. Andrew Murray, *Absolute Surrender: The Blessedness of Forsaking All and Following Christ* (Abbotsford, WI: Aneko, 2017), loc. 128 of 2,394.
2. Leona Choy, *Andrew Murray: The Authorized Biography* (Fort Washington, PA: CLC, 2017), 117.
3. A. W. Tozer, *The Pursuit of God* (Camp Hill, PA: Christian Publications, 1993), 15.

Chapter 2: Returning to Reverence

1. Colby Wedgeworth, Ethan Hulse, and Danny Gokey, "Haven't Seen It Yet," track 3 on Danny Gokey, *Haven't Seen It Yet*, 2019.
2. Murray, *Waiting on God* (Ada, MI: Bethany, 2001), 20.

Chapter 3: The Isaac Altar

1. Francois Fénelon, *Dialogues of Fénelon*, vol. 1 (Mount Morris, NY: Lamplighter, 2018), 63.
2. Rest, peace, calm, tranquility. See Dictionary.com, s.v. "Repose," https://www.dictionary.com/browse/repose?s=t (accessed July 1, 2020).
3. *Dialogues of Fénelon*, 59–60.
4. Murray, *Abide in Christ: A 31-Day Devotional for Fellowship with Jesus* (Apollo, PA: Icthus, 2018), 16.
5. Choy, *Andrew Murray*, 108.
6. Samuel Chadwick, *The Way to Pentecost* (Yuma, CO: Jawbone Digital, 2016), 123.
7. Tozer, *The Pursuit of God*, 15.
8. Ibid., 13–14.
9. Murray, *Absolute Surrender*, loc. 44 of 2,394.

Chapter 4: Fasting in Pursuit

1. The fasting from food discussed in this book is not for everyone. Consult your physician before beginning. Expectant mothers, diabetics, and those with a history of medical problems should maintain essential diets. For those who should not fast from food, it is possible to enter into the attitude of fasting by abstaining from alternatives such as entertainment, social media, the news, or anything God may ask us to set aside for a time to better focus on Him.

2. John Piper, *A Hunger for God: Desiring God Through Fasting and Prayer* (Wheaton, IL: Crossway, 2013), 14.
3. Ibid.
4. Ibid., 25.
5. Ibid., 12.

Chapter 5: Voice Recognition

1. Dr. Jerry Rueb, *Defending the Flock of God: Unmasking the Threat of False Teaching* (Long Beach, CA: Jerry Rueb, 2019), 38.
2. Ibid., 39, 45–46, 49, 52–53.

Chapter 6: Checking the Mute Button

1. Dallas Willard, *Renovation of the Heart: Putting on the Character of Christ* (Colorado Springs: NavPress, 2012), 204.
2. Marcus Aurelius in *Timeless Inspiration: Classic Quotes That Span the Ages* flip calendar (Grand Rapids: Zondervan, 1994), entry for August 17.
3. Murray, *Abide in Christ*, 92.

Chapter 7: Whispers Silence Fear

1. Murray, *Abide in Christ*, 96.
2. Fénelon, *Dialogues of Fénelon*, 53.
3. Murray, *Abide in Christ*, 99.

Chapter 8: Whispers Purify Desires

1. J. C. Ryle, *Holiness: Its Nature, Hindrances, Difficulties and Roots* (London: Pantianos Classics, 2017), v.
2. Murray, *Abide in Christ*, 98.
3. Isobel Kuhn, *By Searching: My Journey Through Doubt into Faith* (Chicago: Moody, 1959), 43.
4. Ibid., 43–44.
5. Murray, *Abide in Christ*, 105.

Chapter 9: Whispers Produce Fruit

1. Murray, *Abide in Christ*, 32–33.
2. Murray, *Waiting on God*, 35.
3. Ibid.
4. Murray, *Abide in Christ*, 138.
5. Henrietta C. Mears in *Timeless Inspiration*, entry for May 18.
6. Murray, *Abide in Christ*, 43.
7. Ibid., 50.
8. Jodie Berndt, *Praying the Scriptures for Your Children: Discover How to Pray God's Purpose for Their Lives* (Grand Rapids: Zondervan, 2001), 41.
9. Dictionary.com, s.v. "Remain," https://www.dictionary.com/browse/remain?s=t (accessed July 2, 2020).
10. Murray, *Abide in Christ*, 35.

Chapter 10: Whispers Lighten Loads

1. *Dialogues of Fénelon*, 71.
2. Murray, *Abide in Christ*, 98.
3. Willard, *Renovation of the Heart*, 175.

4. Ibid., 174.
5. Ibid., 172–173.
6. Ibid., 175.
7. Murray, *Abide in Christ*, 141.
8. Sally Lloyd-Jones, *The Jesus Storybook Bible: Every Story Whispers His Name* (Grand Rapids: Zonderkidz, 2007), 294.

Chapter 11: Whispers Direct Steps

1. Francis Chan, *Letters to the Church* (Colorado Springs: Cook, 2018), 39.
2. Willard, *Renovation of the Heart*, 221.

Chapter 12: Whispers Renew Perspectives

1. Choy, *Andrew Murray*, 79.

Read more about Lisa's story and meet her
Medical Director, Jesus Christ, who walks beside us
in our pain and imparts to us His peace.

PARAKALEO
PRESS

JOURNALING NOTES